skinnytaste®
AIR FRYER DINNERS

75 HEALTHY RECIPES for Easy Weeknight Meals

skinnytaste®
AIR FRYER DINNERS

Gina Homolka

with Heather K. Jones, R.D.

Photographs by Aubrie Pick

CLARKSON POTTER/PUBLISHERS
NEW YORK

CONTENTS

INTRODUCTION

Clearly I'm obsessed with my air fryer since I am now back with a second cookbook solely dedicated to the appliance! When I wrote my first air fryer cookbook in 2019, I was new to the air fryer and had a blast exploring all the possibilities (and making it through failed recipes along the way). Now, it's one of my most-used appliances (along with my coffee pot), and I've learned so much about how to perfect the recipes I make in it. My first air fryer cookbook showcased everything from muffins to appetizers, main dishes, and desserts. This time around, I've honed in on my favorite way to use the air fryer: for outrageously delicious and healthy dinners. This dinner-only air fryer cookbook is packed with flavorful meals that your family is sure to love.

But what is an air fryer anyway? Basically, an air fryer is a countertop convection oven, deep fryer, and microwave all rolled into one. It has a heated coil (usually at the top), a mesh or metal basket to put food in, and a fan that circulates heat around the food in the basket. In an oven, food creates steam that can make things soggy rather than crisp. When deep-frying, items are flash-cooked in hot oil that creates the crunchy exterior we love. An air fryer is the best of both worlds, creating intense heat that surrounds food to cook it more efficiently and evenly than either baking or traditional frying. The result is food with crisp, browned exteriors and juicy, tender interiors. Since you don't have to deal with a big pot of piping hot oil, it's much safer and cleaner than deep-frying (I don't have

to worry about watching my eleven-year-old daughter when she uses it)—not to mention healthier. Mimicking fried foods isn't its only strength, though: The air fryer can roast vegetables and fish, bake muffins and quiche, reheat leftovers, and heat up frozen foods all without warming up your kitchen or requiring preheating (especially helpful in the summer months). It really is a miracle appliance!

I love using my air fryer to make healthier versions of my kids' favorite foods. In this book, I tackled some otherwise high-cal foods like chicken fried steak, samosas, and fried fish sandwiches, just to name a few. I also discovered you can use an air fryer to make stir-fry dishes like Beef and Broccoli (page 106) or Honey Sriracha Chicken and Vegetables (page 77), but without all the splatter. You can also create one-pan dishes similar to sheet pan meals, like One-Pot Balsamic Chicken, Asparagus, and Burst Tomatoes (page 78) or Kielbasa, Veggie, and Pierogi Dinner (page 66) that you simply dump in the basket and cook all together. Of course, the air fryer can also cook up protein like salmon, a whole chicken, juicy pork chops, and steaks in minutes! It's a total game changer for weeknight cooking.

Each recipe in this book includes nutrition information as well as a recipe key labeling recipes that take less than 30 minutes or are gluten-free, dairy-free, vegetarian, or freezer-friendly. I hope this book and the air fryer itself will inspire your weeknight dinners. Have fun with it and be prepared to fall in love. I guarantee you'll find ways to come back to your air fryer time and time again!

AIR FRYER ESSENTIALS

The hands-off approach to air-frying is what makes this awesome appliance so easy to use. With these helpful tips and tricks, you'll create the best overall texture and flavor for your finished dishes.

Flip halfway. The heating element is at the top of the air fryer, so in most cases, you should flip your food halfway through cooking. One common exception is fish, which cooks fine without flipping.

Shake it. For smaller foods, like fries or shrimp, open the fryer and shake the basket halfway through cooking for even results. The cooking time will pause and then resume where you left off once you close the fryer.

Don't overfill. Air fryers work by circulating hot air around food, so if the basket is packed full, it's hard to get the air to flow. This will cause your food to steam (instead of crisp) and cook unevenly. That said, you can use this to your benefit, like I did for the Beef and Broccoli (page 106), where I wanted to steam the veggies.

Make it fit. If your steak or pork loin is too large for the basket, you can cut the meat in half to make it fit, or you can cook the food in batches.

Brown it better. Steaks, chops, and vegetables will brown better when spritzed with a little oil. Fat promotes browning, and a little can go a long way. Pat steaks and chops with paper towels to get rid of excess moisture, to help them brown. Adding a dry rub to leaner steaks and chops helps with overall color.

Be careful with parchment. Don't preheat the air fryer with parchment paper only (it must have food on it!) or it will blow around and catch fire when it touches the heating element.

AIR FRYER Q & A

Here are the most common questions I get about how to choose and use an air fryer.

What is your favorite air fryer?

There are many different types of air fryers out there, from basket-style to toaster oven–style, and even some electric pressure cookers have an air-frying option. I've tried and tested many air fryers, and I really love the basket-style. When purchasing an air fryer with a basket, look for one that's at least 1700 watts, nonstick (it's so easy to clean!), has the ability to adjust both temperature and time, and has a large enough basket that makes sense for your family.

All the recipes in this book have been tested with the GoWISE air fryer with a 5.8-quart basket. This basket will fit a whole chicken, a turkey breast, and other large cuts of meat.

Do I need to preheat the air fryer?

With a few exceptions, the recipes in this book don't require preheating. The air fryer heats much faster than an oven, so it's really not necessary unless you're cooking something that doesn't take long to cook, such as the Sesame-Crusted Tuna with Wasabi Mayo (page 118). Plus, skipping the preheating saves time.

Do you need to add oil?

When air-frying foods that have breading or flour, spritzing the food lightly with oil will help the food get golden and crisp. A little goes a long way. Same with roasting vegetables or making fries—I like to toss the veggies with just enough oil to make the food crisp and moist. In most cases, I usually spray the basket with oil as well to prevent the food from sticking. To prevent buildup and residue that will ruin the basket, look for oil sprays that are both propellant- and additive-free—or purchase an oil mister and fill it with your favorite oil.

How do you clean your air fryer?

It's important to clean your air fryer after each use. Most removable parts of the air fryer, such as the drawer and basket of many models, are dishwasher-safe—but always consult your air fryer manual first before putting parts in the dishwasher. Make sure your air fryer is completely cool before cleaning the inside. The main body of the air fryer and the inside should be wiped with a damp cloth, as grease and food splatters can build up around the heating element and cause smoking. After you clean the air fryer, run it with the empty basket for 1 to 2 minutes to dry out the inside.

Do I need to purchase extras or attachments?

Some air fryers come with racks and pans (or they can be purchased separately), but most of the recipes in this book will not require them. The only extra I used in a few of the recipes is air fryer parchment paper (see next question). For foods that tend to fly around, like the plantain pieces in my jibarito recipe (page 40), I used the rack to hold them down.

Can you use parchment in the air fryer?

Yes, but regular parchment paper doesn't work, because it blocks the flow of air. You should buy air fryer parchment that has holes punched out for air flow (look for it on Amazon). I highly recommend buying a pack to keep on hand for foods that typically stick, like the Spicy Fried Chicken Crunch Wraps (page 82).

Can you use foil in the air fryer?

I use foil only when I want to create a foil sling for lifting out certain foods more easily, especially fish that will break if you try lifting it with a spatula. Or if I am melting cheese over nachos at the very end as I do with Loaded Black Bean Nachos (page 27).

How can I convert recipes that use the regular oven to the air fryer?

A good rule of thumb is to start testing by reducing the temp by 25°F and cutting the cook time in half. Then adjust as needed—it's usually trial and error.

Will the cooking time change depending on how much food is in the basket?

Yes! If I'm making My Signature Wings (page 46), for example, and decide to cook them all in one batch, instead of two as mentioned, even though I shake the basket quite a few times it will usually take almost twice the time to cook. If I'm making just one serving of a recipe with less food in the basket, it will usually take a few minutes less to cook.

RECIPE KEY

Look for these helpful icons throughout the book:

- **Q** Quick (ready in 30 minutes or less)
- **V** Vegetarian
- **GF** Gluten-Free
- **DF** Dairy-Free
- **FF** Freezer-Friendly

WW POINTS

For those of you on WW, all of the up-to-date WW Points are conveniently located on my website under the cookbook tab: Skinnytaste.com/cookbook-index.

A NOTE ABOUT SALT

Different brands and different types of salt vary not only in the amount of sodium per measured amount, but also in the taste. For consistency in my recipes—both for flavor and for the sodium values listed with the recipes—I use Diamond Crystal kosher salt. If you use another type of salt or a different brand of kosher salt, just remember to taste as you go. If you're on a low-sodium diet, feel free to adjust the salt as needed.

VEGGIE MAINS

VEGGIE-LOADED STROMBOLI

SERVES 4

A stromboli is basically a stuffed pizza—and trust me, a stuffed pizza is REALLY good! Many years ago, my cousin lived near a restaurant that only served stromboli. They were stuffed with everything from deli meats and cheese to cheesesteaks or cheeseburgers. We loved going there, and I usually invented my own mix-and-match creation just like this one. Making this veggie stromboli took me back in time, and I ate way too many while testing the recipe—it's just that delicious! This dish is filling on its own, but you can make the meal more substantial with a big green salad on the side.

DOUGH

1 cup (5 ounces) all-purpose or white whole wheat flour, plus more for dusting

1½ teaspoons baking powder

½ teaspoon kosher salt

1 cup (7½ ounces) 0% Greek yogurt, drained if there's any liquid (see Skinny Scoop)

FILLING

1 cup (4 ounces) shredded part-skim mozzarella cheese

1 cup chopped baby spinach

½ cup finely chopped broccoli

¼ cup chopped onion

¼ cup drained chopped roasted red peppers or fresh red bell pepper

½ cup marinara sauce (store-bought or homemade), plus more (optional) for serving

½ cup freshly grated Parmesan or Pecorino Romano cheese

FOR THE DOUGH: In a medium bowl, combine the flour, baking powder, and salt and whisk well. Add the yogurt and mix with a fork or spatula until well combined; it should look like small crumbles.

Transfer the dough to a lightly floured work surface. Knead the dough a few times until the dough is smooth with no lumps, about 20 turns. It will be tacky, but not sticky (it should not leave dough on your hand when you pull away).

Divide the dough into 4 equal balls (about 3½ ounces each). Sprinkle the work surface and a rolling pin with more flour and roll out each ball of dough into thin rounds, 9 inches in diameter.

FOR THE FILLING: Sprinkle ¼ cup mozzarella across the center of each round (avoid starting or ending with sauce or it will be too wet). Top each with ¼ cup baby spinach, 2 tablespoons broccoli, 1 tablespoon each of onion and red pepper, and 2 tablespoons marinara. Sprinkle each with 2 tablespoons Parmesan. Fold one side of the round over the filling to enclose it, tuck the ends in, and fold the other side over to cover the filling. Turn the roll over so that it lies seam-side down on the cutting board. Poke 4 holes on the top with a knife to vent.

Working in batches if needed, place the stromboli in the air fryer basket. Cook at 360°F until puffed and golden, about 8 minutes, flipping halfway through.

Serve the stromboli with additional marinara sauce for dipping, if desired.

Skinny Scoop: Thick Greek yogurt is a must for making this dough. Regular yogurt is too thin and the dough will be too sticky to work with. Some brands may not work, but I always have success with Stonyfield 0% Fat or Fage Total 0%.

PER SERVING: **1 stromboli** · CALORIES **305** · FAT **9.5 g** · SATURATED FAT **5 g** · CHOLESTEROL **32 mg** · CARBOHYDRATE **34 g** · FIBER **2 g** · PROTEIN **20 g** · SUGARS **4 g** · SODIUM **841 mg**

SESAME-SOY TOFU BROCCOLI BOWLS

SERVES 2

1 (14-ounce) package extra-firm tofu

¼ cup reduced-sodium soy sauce or gluten-free tamari

1½ tablespoons honey

1 tablespoon unseasoned rice vinegar

2 teaspoons sambal oelek or Sriracha

2 teaspoons toasted sesame oil

Olive oil spray

½ teaspoon cornstarch

1 teaspoon grated fresh ginger

FOR SERVING

1½ cups cooked brown rice

1 cup steamed broccoli florets (fresh or frozen; see Skinny Scoop)

2 medium scallions, sliced

½ teaspoon sesame seeds

Tofu is a great source of plant-based protein, but even as a meat eater, I still love to eat it—and crisping it up in the air fryer couldn't be easier! Plain tofu can be bland, but it soaks up the flavors of whatever you marinate it in. I love the salty, sweet, and spicy combo of this simple marinade made with soy sauce, honey, and the Indonesian chile paste sambal oelek.

Place the tofu block between some paper towels and press to absorb excess water. Repeat until the tofu feels dry and no more water comes out. Slice the tofu into 1-inch cubes.

In a medium bowl, stir together the soy sauce, honey, rice vinegar, sambal oelek, and sesame oil. Add the tofu and marinate for 20 to 30 minutes (any longer and it will soak up the marinade needed for the sauce).

Spritz the air fryer basket with oil. Remove the tofu from the marinade and set the sauce aside. Working in batches if needed, add the tofu to the air fryer basket in a single layer. Cook at 370°F until the tofu is slightly golden and crisp on the outside and slightly chewy on the inside, 12 to 15 minutes, flipping halfway through.

Transfer the reserved marinade to a nonstick medium skillet. Add the cornstarch, ginger, and 2 tablespoons water and whisk to combine. Cook over medium-low heat and bring to a boil. Cook until the mixture has thickened, 30 seconds to 1 minute (be careful not to let it dry up). Remove the skillet from the heat. Add the tofu to the reduced sauce and toss until evenly coated.

TO SERVE: Divide the brown rice and broccoli between two bowls and top with the tofu and sauce. Garnish with the scallions and sesame seeds and serve immediately.

Skinny Scoop: Quickly steam fresh broccoli in the microwave by adding 1 tablespoon water to a microwave-safe container and cooking, partially covered, for 1 to 2 minutes.

PER SERVING: 1 bowl · CALORIES 496 · FAT 19 g · SATURATED FAT 2 g · CHOLESTEROL 0 mg · CARBOHYDRATE 62 g · FIBER 8.5 g · PROTEIN 28 g · SUGARS 17 g · SODIUM 1,244 mg

HERBY TOFU SUMMER ROLLS
WITH PEANUT SAUCE

SERVES 4

24 large butter lettuce leaves, from 2 heads (save the small inner leaves for another use)

1 (12-ounce) package extra-firm tofu

1 teaspoon toasted sesame oil

½ teaspoon kosher salt

½ teaspoon freshly ground black pepper

3 tablespoons hoisin sauce*

3 tablespoons smooth peanut butter

1 teaspoon grated fresh ginger

¼ cup very hot water, plus more for the rice paper

Olive oil spray

12 (8½-inch) rice paper wrappers

3 cups shredded carrots

1 large English cucumber, quartered crosswise and cut into matchsticks (about 2½ cups)

¾ cup loosely packed fresh mint leaves

1 cup fresh cilantro sprigs, tough stems removed

*Read the label to be sure this product is gluten-free.

Vietnamese-style summer rolls are so fresh and flavorful! My biggest tip is to have your ingredients prepped before you assemble the rolls. That way, the rice paper won't dry out, which makes them hard to work with. The rolling may take a little practice, so don't feel bad if your first few attempts fail!

Remove any tough bottom parts of the lettuce leaves that might tear the rice paper.

Place the tofu block between some paper towels and press to absorb excess water. Repeat until the tofu feels dry and no more water comes out. Cut the tofu into thirds lengthwise so you have three long rectangles. Cut each rectangle into 8 cubes to give you 24 cubes total. Put the tofu in a large bowl with the sesame oil, salt, and pepper and toss very gently to coat.

In a medium bowl, combine the hoisin, peanut butter, ginger, and hot water. Stir until the sauce is smooth and shiny. Measure out ½ cup to use as a dipping sauce for serving, leaving the remaining 2½ tablespoons in the bowl.

Spritz the air fryer basket with oil. Working in batches if needed, add the tofu to the basket in a single layer, avoiding any overlap as much as possible. Cook at 400°F until the tofu is heated through, 8 to 10 minutes, gently flipping halfway through. Transfer the tofu to the bowl with the reserved peanut sauce and toss to coat.

Place about ½ cup hot tap water in a large, shallow bowl. Take a rice paper wrapper and completely submerge it in the hot water 10 to 15 seconds, until the wrapper is pliable.

Place the wrapper on a plate or plastic cutting board and top with 2 lettuce leaves, 2 cubes of tofu, ¼ cup carrots, a little less of the cucumber, 3 to 4 mint leaves, and 1 cilantro sprig.

Fold the bottom half of the wrapper over the filling, hold the fold in place, tuck in the sides, and roll tightly. Set aside. Repeat with the remaining wrappers and fillings and serve with the peanut sauce for dipping.

PER SERVING: **3 rolls + 2 tablespoons sauce** • CALORIES **394** • FAT **13 g** • SATURATED FAT **2.5 g** • CHOLESTEROL **0 mg** • CARBOHYDRATE **54 g** • FIBER **7.5 g** • PROTEIN **17 g** • SUGARS **11 g** • SODIUM **611 mg**

BIG GREEN SALAD
WITH CRISPY SPICED CHICKPEAS AND HALLOUMI

SERVES 4

CHICKPEAS
1 (15-ounce) can chickpeas*

Olive oil spray

¼ teaspoon sweet paprika

¼ teaspoon ground cumin

⅛ teaspoon kosher salt

DRESSING
¼ cup fresh lemon juice

1 tablespoon dried oregano

1 garlic clove, grated

½ teaspoon kosher salt

2 tablespoons extra-virgin olive oil

SALAD
4 ounces Halloumi cheese, cut into 8 pieces

7 cups chopped romaine lettuce (about 1 large head)

2½ cups chopped English cucumber (about 1 large)

1 pint cherry tomatoes, halved

20 pitted Kalamata olives, roughly chopped

4 sliced scallions

On nights when all I crave is a big, hearty green salad, this chopped Greek salad totally fits the bill. It's loaded with romaine, cucumbers, tomatoes, olives, and scallions all tossed in a really oregano-y dressing that's *so good* you'll want to make it again and again. Finished with crispy air-fried spiced chickpeas and Halloumi for protein, texture, and (of course!) taste, this is a delicious and filling main-dish salad that won't disappoint.

FOR THE CHICKPEAS: Drain and rinse the chickpeas in a colander or salad spinner and transfer to a plate lined with paper towels. Allow to dry completely.

When the chickpeas are dry, preheat the air fryer to 380°F. Spritz the basket with oil. Working in batches if needed, add the chickpeas to the air fryer basket in a single layer and cook, shaking the basket every 5 minutes, until the chickpeas are crunchy and golden brown on the outside, about 12 minutes.

Meanwhile, in a small bowl, combine the paprika, cumin, and salt.

Transfer the chickpeas to a medium bowl, spritz all over with oil, and immediately toss with the spice mixture while hot.

FOR THE DRESSING: In a small bowl, combine the lemon juice, oregano, garlic, and salt and let sit until the oregano has absorbed some liquid, about 5 minutes. Whisk in the olive oil.

FOR THE SALAD: Increase the air fryer temperature to 400°F. Working in batches if needed, add the Halloumi to the air fryer basket in a single layer and cook for 1 minute. Flip and cook until golden brown and slightly softened, about 1 minute more. Transfer the cheese to a plate to let cool and firm up for a few minutes while you assemble the salad.

In a large bowl, combine the romaine, cucumber, tomatoes, olives, and scallions. Drizzle the dressing over the salad, toss, and divide among four bowls. Top each bowl with one-quarter of the chickpeas and 2 slices of Halloumi and serve.

*Read the label to be sure this product is gluten-free.

PER SERVING: 3 cups • CALORIES 318 • FAT 18 g • SATURATED FAT 6.5 g • CHOLESTEROL 25 mg • CARBOHYDRATE 29 g • FIBER 8 g • PROTEIN 14 g • SUGARS 7 g • SODIUM 834 mg

EGGPLANT PARMESAN

SERVES 4

1/2 cup part-skim
ricotta cheese

6 tablespoons shredded
part-skim mozzarella cheese*

1/4 cup freshly grated
Pecorino Romano or
Parmesan cheese

2 tablespoons finely chopped
fresh parsley, plus more
(optional) for garnish

2 medium eggplants
(about 14 ounces each)

1/2 teaspoon kosher salt

Freshly ground black pepper

2 large eggs

1 cup seasoned bread crumbs,
whole wheat or gluten-free

Olive oil spray

1 1/2 cups marinara
sauce (store-bought or
homemade), warmed

*Read the label to be sure
this product is gluten-free.

Eggplant Parmesan is one of those dishes that grew on me through the years. As a kid, I was never a fan, but now I actually crave it! My Italian sister-in-law makes the best fried version of this dish, but I put my air fryer to the test and the result was crispy breaded eggplant, cozy marinara sauce, and gooey melted cheese—what's not to love? Serve this with a big green salad, spiralized zucchini, or some pasta on the side.

In a medium bowl, combine the ricotta, mozzarella, Parmesan, and parsley.

Slice the smaller ends off the eggplant and cut the eggplants into 12 rounds 3/4 inch thick. Season the eggplant with the salt and pepper to taste. In a shallow bowl, beat the eggs with 1 teaspoon water. Place the bread crumbs in another bowl or plate.

Dredge each eggplant slice in the egg, letting any excess drip off, then dredge in the bread crumbs. Spritz each slice on both sides with a generous amount of oil.

Working in batches if needed, arrange the eggplant in the air fryer basket in a single layer. Cook at 380°F until crisp and golden on the outside and tender in the center, about 12 minutes, flipping halfway through. Transfer the eggplant to a large plate.

Set aside 1/2 cup marinara for serving. Spoon 1 generous tablespoon of the remaining marinara and 1 tablespoon of the cheese mixture on top of each eggplant round. Working in batches again, return the eggplant in a single layer to the air fryer basket and reduce the temperature to 350°F. Cook until the cheese has melted, 1 to 2 minutes.

To serve, ladle the reserved marinara sauce onto plates and top with the eggplant. Garnish with the additional parsley, if desired.

PER SERVING: **3 pieces** · CALORIES **288** · FAT **11 g** · SATURATED FAT **5 g** · CHOLESTEROL **115 mg** ·
CARBOHYDRATE **33 g** · FIBER **8.5 g** · PROTEIN **16 g** · SUGARS **10 g** · SODIUM **939 mg**

UN-FRIED FALAFEL

SERVES 4

1 (15.5-ounce) can chickpeas, rinsed and drained

1 small yellow onion, quartered

3 garlic cloves, roughly chopped

1/3 cup roughly chopped fresh parsley

1/3 cup roughly chopped fresh cilantro

1/3 cup chopped scallions

1 teaspoon ground cumin

1/2 teaspoon kosher salt

1/8 teaspoon crushed red pepper flakes

1 teaspoon baking powder

1/4 cup all-purpose flour, plus more for dusting

Olive oil spray

FOR SERVING (OPTIONAL)

Pita

Hummus

Tahini

Sliced tomatoes

Sliced cucumber

Thinly sliced red onion

Falafel is a delicious Middle Eastern vegetarian dish made with chickpeas, onions, and a mix of herbs and spices. I wanted to create a falafel recipe made from canned chickpeas that was quick, easy, and didn't require deep-frying. So, naturally, the air fryer came to the rescue! These falafel are protein-packed, nutritious, and light—perfect on days when you want to go meatless, or if you just want to include more plant-based foods in your diet. Serve them in a pita, over hummus, or with couscous or rice—you decide!

Pat the chickpeas with paper towels to dry.

In a food processor, combine the onion and garlic and pulse a few times until roughly chopped. Add the parsley, cilantro, scallions, cumin, salt, and pepper flakes. Pulse until well blended, 30 to 60 seconds. Add the chickpeas and pulse 2 to 3 times more until just blended but still slightly chunky, not pureed.

Add the baking powder and flour, scrape the sides of the bowl down with a spatula, and pulse 2 to 3 times until just combined. Transfer the mixture to a large bowl, cover, and refrigerate for 2 to 3 hours or freeze for 20 minutes.

Form the falafel mixture into 12 balls. (If it's too sticky, lightly dust your hands with flour.)

Preheat the air fryer to 350°F.

Spritz the falafel with oil. Working in batches, add the falafel to the air fryer basket in a single layer. Cook until golden brown and crisp, about 14 minutes flipping halfway through.

TO SERVE: If desired, to make this a meal, serve the falafel in a pita with hummus, tahini, sliced tomatoes, cucumber, and red onion.

PER SERVING: 3 balls · CALORIES 165 · FAT 2 g · SATURATED FAT 0 g · CHOLESTEROL 0 mg · CARBOHYDRATE 32 g · FIBER 5 g · PROTEIN 7 g · SUGARS 7 g · SODIUM 491 mg

LOADED BLACK BEAN NACHOS

SERVES 4

12 (6-inch) corn tortillas

Olive oil spray

1 teaspoon chili powder*

1 teaspoon kosher salt

1 cup canned fat-free refried black beans*

1 tablespoon chipotle hot sauce, such as Cholula

1 tablespoon fresh lime juice

1 (15-ounce) can black beans, rinsed and drained, or 1½ cups cooked black beans

¾ cup chunky jarred salsa

½ cup shredded Mexican cheese blend*

1 fresh jalapeño pepper, thinly sliced (optional)

¼ cup chopped fresh cilantro

¼ cup light sour cream

1 avocado, sliced (optional)

*Read the label to be sure this product is gluten-free.

Skinny Scoop: For the refried beans, check the label and choose brands with just a few ingredients: beans, water, and maybe salt.

Winner, winner, nacho dinner! This is a fun, crowd-pleasing vegetarian entree that's not only filling (thanks to two types of beans!) but also feels indulgent. The air fryer turns tortillas into super-crunchy fresh chips, and the store-bought refried beans are magically transformed into a creamy sauce that replaces nacho cheese.

Preheat the air fryer to 350°F.

Stack the tortillas and cut them into 8 wedges (as you would cut a pizza). Add the slices to a large bowl and spritz with oil. Add the chili powder and salt and toss to coat.

Working in batches if needed, add the tortillas to the air fryer basket in a single layer and cook until crisp and golden, 5 to 9 minutes, shaking the basket halfway through to keep them from sticking to one another. Set aside to cool.

Meanwhile, in a medium bowl, combine the refried beans, hot sauce, and lime juice and stir to coat. Thin out the mixture with just enough water (about 2 tablespoons) so that the beans can be easily dolloped with a spoon.

In a bowl, combine the black beans with ¼ cup of the salsa.

Line the air fryer basket with foil to create a sling so the food will be easy to lift out. Working in about two batches, add half the tortilla chips, half of the refried bean mixture, and half of the black bean/salsa mixture, layering as you go. Top with half the shredded cheese and half the jalapeño slices (if using). Increase the air fryer temperature to 370°F and cook until the cheese is melted, 3 to 4 minutes. Lift the foil sling to transfer the nachos to a plate and repeat with the remaining ingredients for the second batch.

Spoon the remaining ½ cup salsa all over the nachos and sprinkle with the cilantro. In a small bowl, thin the sour cream with 1 to 2 tablespoons water until it is thin enough to drizzle. Top the nachos with the sour cream drizzle and the sliced avocado (if using). Serve warm.

PER SERVING: **24 loaded chips** · CALORIES **379** · FAT **8 g** · SATURATED FAT **4 g** · CHOLESTEROL **19 mg** · CARBOHYDRATE **61 g** · FIBER **16 g** · PROTEIN **18 g** · SUGARS **3 g** · SODIUM **1,135 mg**

GIANT SAMOSAS
WITH CILANTRO-MINT CHUTNEY

SERVES 6

SAMOSAS

1 (8.7-ounce) sheet frozen puff pastry, thawed

1 pound Yukon Gold potatoes, peeled and cut into 1-inch pieces

12 ounces cauliflower florets (about ½ medium head), cut into bite-size pieces

2 teaspoons garam masala

1 teaspoon ground cumin

¼ teaspoon cayenne pepper, or more to taste

2 teaspoons kosher salt

1 tablespoon unsalted butter or ghee

½ medium yellow onion, diced

1 garlic clove, minced

1 tablespoon grated fresh ginger

1 cup frozen green peas, thawed

Juice of ½ lemon

¼ cup chopped fresh cilantro

All-purpose flour, for dusting

1 large egg, beaten

Olive oil spray

A traditional samosa is a potato-stuffed, deep-fried Indian snack. It was also the very first Indian dish I ever tried, many, many moons ago and made by a very kind Indian co-worker! Here, I took the classic Indian dish and made it big enough to enjoy as a meal. I used puff pastry to give the exterior a different texture, and added cauliflower to the filling to lighten it up—trust me, you won't even know the extra vegetables are there (I even fooled Tommy!). Although this dish does take a bit more time to prepare, it is totally worth it. Plus, the samosas freeze and refrigerate well, making them perfect to make ahead. *(See recipe photo on page 2.)*

FOR THE SAMOSAS: Cut the puff pastry along the folds of the sheet into 3 strips, then cut again crosswise to get a total of 6 rectangles.

In a large microwave-safe bowl, combine the potatoes and cauliflower with 2 tablespoons water, cover with a lid, and microwave for 10 minutes, stirring halfway through. Set the bowl aside and keep covered.

In a small bowl, combine the garam masala, cumin, cayenne, and ½ teaspoon of the salt.

In a medium skillet, melt the butter over medium-high heat. Add the onion and cook until starting to brown, about 3 minutes. Add the garlic, ginger, and the spice mixture and cook for 1 minute more. Add the peas, lemon juice, and cilantro and gently stir. Cook 1 minute more to allow the flavors to meld. Set aside.

Line a sheet pan with parchment paper. Lightly dust a clean work surface and a rolling pin with flour. Working with one piece at a time, roll the puff pastry into 7-inch squares, rotating after each pass, to keep the dough in a square shape. Set each aside on the lined sheet pan.

Mash the potato and cauliflower mixture with a potato masher or fork until mostly smooth but still slightly chunky. Add the remaining 1½ teaspoons salt and the onion and pea mixture and stir to combine.

CHUTNEY

½ cup fresh cilantro

½ cup fresh mint leaves, roughly chopped

1-inch piece fresh ginger, peeled and roughly chopped

½ medium yellow onion, roughly chopped

1 small fresh jalapeño pepper, seeds and membranes removed (for less heat), roughly chopped

Juice of ½ lemon

½ teaspoon ground cumin

½ teaspoon kosher salt

¼ cup nonfat plain yogurt

2 to 4 tablespoons water, as needed

Working with 1 square of pastry at a time, place on a clean work surface with the points facing top and bottom like a diamond. Spoon a heaping ½ cup of the filling on the bottom half of the dough and spread the filling in an even layer with your fingers or a fork, leaving a ½-inch border. Brush the edges of the dough with the beaten egg, then fold the dough over itself, pressing the edges with your fingers or a fork to seal. Repeat with the remaining dough and filling, then brush the tops with the egg wash.

Preheat the air fryer to 390°F.

Spritz the basket with oil. Working in batches, add 2 samosas to the air fryer basket and cook until the samosas are golden and crisp, about 10 minutes, flipping halfway through. Repeat with the remaining samosas, spritzing the basket in between batches.

MEANWHILE, FOR THE CHUTNEY: In a blender or food processor, combine all of the chutney ingredients and blend until smooth and combined.

Serve the samosas immediately with the chutney on the side.

PER SERVING: **1 samosa + 3 tablespoons chutney** · CALORIES **366** · FAT **19 g** · SATURATED FAT **5.5 g** · CHOLESTEROL **36 mg** · CARBOHYDRATE **42 g** · FIBER **5.5 g** · PROTEIN **9 g** · SUGARS **5 g** · SODIUM **638 mg**

CHEESY CALZONES

SERVES 4

DOUGH

1 cup (5 ounces) all-purpose or white whole wheat flour, plus more for dusting

1½ teaspoons baking powder

½ teaspoon kosher salt

1 cup (7½ ounces) 0% Greek yogurt, drained if there's any liquid

FILLING

1¼ cups shredded part-skim mozzarella cheese (5 ounces)

¾ cup 2% cottage cheese (I love Good Culture), drained in a mesh sieve

¼ cup freshly grated Pecorino Romano cheese

1 garlic clove, minced

ASSEMBLY AND SERVING

Flour, for dusting

1 large egg, lightly beaten

Sesame seeds (optional)

Olive oil spray

Marinara sauce (store-bought or homemade), warmed for serving (optional)

These are the cheesiest calzones and, shhhh, don't tell my husband that I used cottage cheese in the mix because he had no idea! Calzones are similar to stromboli only they're shaped like half-moons and usually stuffed with ricotta cheese. Here, I skipped the ricotta altogether and used a combo of cottage cheese, mozzarella, and Pecorino Romano to create a high-protein cheesy filling (think white pizza) that's perfect for dunking into some warm marinara.

FOR THE DOUGH: In a medium bowl, combine the flour, baking powder, and salt and whisk well. Add the yogurt and mix with a fork or spatula until well combined; it should look like small crumbles.

Transfer the dough to a lightly floured work surface. Knead the dough a few times until the dough is smooth with no lumps, about 20 turns.

FOR THE FILLING: In a medium bowl, combine the mozzarella, cottage cheese, pecorino, and garlic and mix well.

TO ASSEMBLE: Divide the dough into 4 equal balls (about 3½ ounces each). Sprinkle the work surface and rolling pin with more flour and roll out the dough into thin rounds 8 to 9 inches in diameter.

Spread one-quarter of the cheese mixture evenly over the bottom half of each dough round (about ½ cup for each round), leaving a 1-inch border around the edge. Brush the border with the beaten egg and fold the top over the filling to make a half-moon shape, leaving the bottom ½ inch of the border uncovered. Seal the edges using the tines of a fork. Brush the top with the egg wash and poke a few holes in the top of the calzone with a knife to vent. Sprinkle the calzone all over with sesame seeds, if desired.

Spritz the air fryer basket with olive oil. Working in batches if needed, place the calzones in the air fryer basket in a single layer. Cook at 360°F until golden, about 10 minutes, flipping halfway through. Serve with marinara, if desired.

PER SERVING: 1 calzone · CALORIES 310 · FAT 10.5 g · SATURATED FAT 6 g · CHOLESTEROL 49 mg · CARBOHYDRATE 30 g · FIBER 1 g · PROTEIN 25 g · SUGARS 4 g · SODIUM 807 mg

GENERAL TSO'S CAULIFLOWER

SERVES 4

18 ounces cauliflower (about 1 large head), cut into 1½-inch florets (4 heaping cups)

1 tablespoon plus 1 teaspoon toasted sesame oil

½ teaspoon garlic powder

2 scallions

2½ tablespoons reduced-sodium soy sauce or gluten-free tamari

1 tablespoon cornstarch

¾ cup vegetable broth

2 tablespoons hoisin sauce*

2 tablespoons unseasoned rice vinegar

1 tablespoon Sriracha sauce

1½ teaspoons minced fresh ginger

2 garlic cloves, minced

Toasted sesame seeds, for garnish

Cooked rice, for serving (optional)

*Read the label to be sure this product is gluten-free.

Cauliflower is like a blank canvas that absorbs any seasoning or spice. It's also a nutritional powerhouse packed with vitamin C, fiber, and antioxidants. Here, I transformed a popular Chinese-American restaurant dish, typically made with chicken, into a vegetarian meal that's packed with flavor. By roasting the cauliflower in the air fryer and then finishing it with a quick pan sauce, the whole dish comes together very quickly. Healthy, tasty, *and* ready in under 20 minutes? Always a winning combo!

In a large bowl, combine the cauliflower, 1 tablespoon of the sesame oil, and the garlic powder.

Cut off the scallion greens from the whites. Mince the whites and thinly slice the greens to reserve for garnish.

Working in batches if needed, add the cauliflower to the air fryer basket in a single layer. Cook at 380°F until tender, 7 to 8 minutes, shaking the basket halfway through.

Meanwhile, in a medium bowl, combine the soy sauce and cornstarch, mixing until the cornstarch is dissolved. Add the vegetable broth, hoisin, vinegar, and Sriracha and set aside.

When the cauliflower is cooked, in a large nonstick skillet or wok, heat the remaining 1 teaspoon sesame oil over medium heat. Add the scallion whites, ginger, and garlic and sauté for a minute or so, just until they're fragrant but before they turn brown. Pour in the sauce and bring to a simmer. Cook, stirring, just until the sauce has thickened, 30 to 60 seconds. Remove the skillet from the heat and add the cauliflower directly to the sauce, tossing to coat.

Garnish the cauliflower with the scallion greens and sesame seeds. Serve immediately over rice, if desired.

PER SERVING: **1 generous cup** · CALORIES **122** · FAT **5 g** · SATURATED FAT **1 g** · CHOLESTEROL **0 mg** · CARBOHYDRATE **17 g** · FIBER **4 g** · PROTEIN **4 g** · SUGARS **7 g** · SODIUM **717 mg**

VEGGIE FRENCH BREAD PIZZAS

SERVES 4

8 ounces whole wheat French or Italian bread

1 cup marinara sauce (store-bought or homemade)

⅓ cup sliced red onion

⅓ cup diced green bell pepper

⅓ cup finely chopped steamed broccoli florets (or thawed frozen)

1 cup shredded whole-milk mozzarella cheese (4 ounces), such as Polly-O, or mozzarella-style nondairy cheese

¼ cup freshly grated Parmesan cheese (or nondairy; see Skinny Scoop)

I created this recipe with the kiddos in mind, but to be honest, what adult wouldn't want this delicious French bread pizza? Growing up, French bread pizzas were a staple in our home. My mom always had a few boxes of Stouffer's stashed away in the freezer, and after school if we had friends over, we would pop them in the toaster oven and patiently wait for them to heat up. Making these from scratch is quicker and so much healthier because you can control the ingredients you're using. They take less than 5 minutes to cook in the air fryer and you can top them with whatever pizza toppings you love: mushrooms, pepperoni, sausage, and more.

Cut the bread in half lengthwise, then cut each half crosswise into 2 pieces to give you 4 pieces total.

Spread ¼ cup of the marinara sauce on each piece. Distribute the onion, pepper, and broccoli evenly among the tops of the bread, then sprinkle with the mozzarella and Parmesan.

Working in batches if needed, place the pizzas in the air fryer basket in a single layer. Cook at 370°F until the cheese is melted and bubbling and the bread is crisp, 3 to 4 minutes.

Serve immediately.

Skinny Scoop: I've tested many brands of nondairy cheese and really love the taste of Violife mozzarella-style cheese. If you don't eat dairy, you can omit the Parmesan and use a total of 1¼ cups vegan cheese.

PER SERVING: **1 pizza** · CALORIES **300** · FAT **10 g** · SATURATED FAT **5 g** · CHOLESTEROL **28 mg** · CARBOHYDRATE **38 g** · FIBER **3 g** · PROTEIN **14 g** · SUGARS **5 g** · SODIUM **712 mg**

CAJUN ARANCINI WITH ROASTED RED PEPPER MARINARA

SERVES 4

1 large red bell pepper, cut into ¼-inch-thick strips

1 medium yellow onion, cut into ¼-inch-thick slices

1 teaspoon extra-virgin olive oil

1¾ teaspoons kosher salt

¾ teaspoon cayenne pepper

3 cups marinara sauce (store-bought or homemade)

2 (15-ounce) cans no salt added red beans, rinsed and drained*

2 cups cooked brown rice

2 egg whites

1 celery stalk, finely diced

1 teaspoon garlic powder

1 teaspoon sweet paprika

¾ cup plain fine bread crumbs, wheat or gluten-free

¼ cup freshly grated Parmesan cheese

2½ ounces pepper Jack cheese, cut into sixteen ½-inch cubes

Olive oil spray

2 scallions, green parts only, thinly sliced

1 lemon, cut into wedges, for serving

*Read the label to be sure this product is gluten-free.

I love Italian rice balls, and I love Cajun food, so these Cajun-inspired arancini are a real winner in my book! They're a Cajun and Italian mashup, made with spiced red beans and rice and stuffed with pepper Jack cheese. Serve with a salad on the side, if desired.

In a medium bowl, toss the bell pepper and onion with the olive oil. Season with ¼ teaspoon of the salt and ¼ teaspoon of the cayenne. Arrange the bell pepper and onion in the air fryer basket. Cook at 380°F until the veggies are browned around the edges, 10 to 12 minutes, stirring halfway through.

Transfer the roasted vegetables to a medium saucepan. Add the marinara sauce and cook over medium heat just until the sauce warms through, 3 to 4 minutes. Cover and keep warm.

In a medium bowl, mash the beans with a potato masher or fork until they're creamy but not pulverized. Add the rice, egg whites, celery, garlic powder, paprika, ¼ cup of the bread crumbs, and the remaining 1½ teaspoons salt and the ½ teaspoon cayenne. Stir until everything is incorporated.

In a small bowl, combine the remaining ½ cup bread crumbs with the Parmesan.

Portion and shape the rice mixture into 16 balls (about 3 tablespoons each). Press your thumb into the center of each, making a deep pocket, and stuff a cube of pepper Jack inside. Smooth the rice mixture around the cheese filling and reshape the balls.

Dredge each rice ball in the bread crumb mixture, tossing gently to coat. Spritz the arancini with oil.

Working in batches if needed, arrange the arancini in the air fryer basket in a single layer and spritz the tops with oil. Cook at 400°F until golden brown, 8 to 12 minutes, flipping halfway through.

To serve, ladle the roasted red pepper marinara into four bowls and top each bowl with 4 arancini. Garnish with the scallion greens and a squeeze of lemon.

PER SERVING: 4 balls + ¾ cup sauce · CALORIES 504 · FAT 10 g · SATURATED FAT 4.5 g · CHOLESTEROL 20 mg · CARBOHYDRATE 77 g · FIBER 16 g · PROTEIN 22 g · SUGARS 11 g · SODIUM 1,221 mg

POULTRY

CHICKEN PLANTAIN SANDWICH (JIBARITO DE POLLO)

SERVES 2

A jibarito is a Puerto Rican sandwich that's made with a twice-fried, flattened plantain in place of bread. It's typically made with steak, but I opted for chicken, added some sautéed onions and jalapeño, and rather than use the typical mayo-ketchup spread, I made a quick garlic mayo. Tommy, who's half Puerto Rican, gave this a big thumbs-up! We served it with rice and beans to round out this Latin meal, but of course a salad would work, too.

Kosher salt

3/4 teaspoon garlic powder

2 tablespoons mayonnaise

1 small garlic clove,
finely grated

2 thin sliced chicken breast
cutlets, about 4 ounces
each, 1/4 inch thick

1 teaspoon olive oil

1/2 medium onion,
sliced 1/4 inch thick

1 small jalapeño, sliced
into thin rounds

1 large green plantain

Olive oil spray

2 Romaine lettuce leaves

4 thin slices vine tomato

In a small bowl, combine 1 cup water with 1 teaspoon salt and the garlic powder. In another small bowl, combine the mayonnaise and garlic. Season the chicken with 1/4 teaspoon salt and spread half of the garlic mayo on both sides of the chicken, reserving the other half of the garlic mayo to make the sandwiches.

In a medium skillet over medium heat, combine the olive oil, onion, jalapeño, and a pinch of salt. Cook, stirring occasionally, until tender, about 5 minutes. Set aside.

Meanwhile, with a sharp knife, score a slit along the length of the plantain skin (this will make it easier to peel). Remove the peel, then cut the plantain in half lengthwise, then again crosswise, to make 4 pieces total.

Spritz the plantain pieces all over with olive oil and place in the air fryer basket. Cook at 400°F until tender, about 8 minutes, flipping halfway.

While still hot, place one plantain piece between 2 heavy plastic or wooden cutting boards lined with wax paper. Press or smash to flatten with all your weight so it is very thin (I personally place the boards on the floor and step on them to make the plantain super thin). Repeat with the remaining pieces.

Dip one piece at a time in the seasoned water (discard the water). Generously spray both sides of the plantains with olive oil. Working in batches if needed, transfer to the air fryer basket in a single layer. Cook at 400°F until golden and crisp on both sides, about 6 minutes, flipping halfway. Transfer to a cutting board and immediately give them another spritz of oil and season with 1/8 teaspoon salt.

Place the chicken in the air fryer basket. Cook at 400°F until cooked through, about 6 minutes, flipping halfway.

To serve, top 2 plantain pieces with a lettuce leaf. Top with the chicken, half of the onion-jalapeño mixture, then tomato slices. Spread the remaining mayo on the 2 remaining plantain pieces and place on top to form 2 sandwiches.

Skinny Scoop: If the plantain pieces start to fly around in the air fryer basket while cooking, use a small rack to hold them down.

PER SERVING: 1 sandwich · CALORIES 420 · FAT 16 g · SATURATED FAT 2 g · CHOLESTEROL 93 mg · CARBOHYDRATE 42 g · FIBER 4.5 g · PROTEIN 28 g · SUGARS 20 g · SODIUM 401 mg

PISTACHIO-CRUSTED CHICKEN CUTLETS

SERVES 4

1 lemon

1 cup raw unsalted pistachios (4¼ ounces)

2 boneless, skinless chicken breasts (1 pound)

Kosher salt and freshly ground black pepper

Olive oil spray

6 cups baby arugula

1 tablespoon extra-virgin olive oil

2 ounces shaved Parmesan cheese

Pistachios are without a doubt my favorite nut, and using them to crust chicken cutlets, you just can't go wrong! Served with a simple arugula salad, this dish is easy enough for a weeknight but feels fancy enough for a dinner party. If you can't find unsalted raw nuts, omit the salt in the recipe and use salted. When you chop the nuts in the food processor, be sure to make it chunky like a coarse crumb. If the nuts are too large, they won't stick to the chicken, but if you overprocess them, they will turn into a fine flour or paste, which won't work, either.

Grate the zest from half of the lemon and place on a large plate. Juice half the lemon and then cut the other half into wedges. Set both aside.

In a food processor, pulse the pistachios a few times until it becomes a coarse crumb, being careful not to overprocess. Transfer to the plate with the lemon zest, mix, and set aside.

Slice the chicken breasts in half horizontally to make 4 thin cutlets. Place each cutlet between two sheets of parchment and pound with a mallet to a ¼-inch thickness. Season with 1 teaspoon salt and pepper to taste.

One at a time, press the chicken cutlets into the pistachio/lemon zest mixture until completely covered on both sides. Spritz both sides with olive oil spray.

Working in batches if needed, place the chicken cutlets in the air fryer basket in a single layer. Cook at 380°F until the chicken is cooked through in the center, flipping once, 3 minutes per side.

Meanwhile, in a large bowl, toss together the arugula, olive oil, reserved lemon juice, a pinch of salt, and black pepper to taste.

Divide the arugula among four plates and top with the Parmesan. Set a chicken cutlet alongside and serve with the lemon wedges.

PER SERVING: 1 cutlet + 1½ cups salad · CALORIES 403 · FAT 24 g · SATURATED FAT 5 g · CHOLESTEROL 92 mg · CARBOHYDRATE 11 g · FIBER 3.5 g · PROTEIN 38 g · SUGARS 3 g · SODIUM 644 mg

HONEY MUSTARD CHICKEN TENDERS

SERVES 4

12 chicken tenderloins
(about 24 ounces total;
see Skinny Scoop)

¼ teaspoon kosher salt

4 tablespoons Dijon mustard

3 tablespoons honey

3 tablespoons light
mayonnaise

1 teaspoon fresh lemon juice

½ cup seasoned bread
crumbs, wheat or gluten-free

½ cup plain panko bread
crumbs, wheat or gluten-free

Olive oil spray

Tommy loves chicken tenders with honey mustard, so I set out to make a healthier version of his fast-food favorite. The honey mustard sauce needs time in the refrigerator to let the flavors meld, so I prefer starting it the night before and marinating the chicken in some of the sauce. No need to add eggs here, since the crumbs stick perfectly without. I love serving chicken tenders with a big green salad on the side, but for something more substantial, they're perfect with Savory Sweet Potato Wedges (page 167) or Lemon Potatoes (page 168).

In a large bowl, season the chicken with the salt. In a small bowl, combine the mustard, honey, mayonnaise, and lemon juice and mix well. Use 2 tablespoons of the honey mustard to rub all over the chicken. Cover both the chicken and the remaining sauce and refrigerate for at least 8 and up to 12 hours.

In a shallow bowl, combine the seasoned bread crumbs and panko. Working in batches, dip the chicken into the bread crumb mixture, pressing to adhere. Shake off any excess and place on a large plate or cutting board. Spritz both sides of the chicken generously with oil.

Preheat the air fryer to 400°F.

Working in batches if needed, place the chicken in the air fryer basket in a single layer. Cook until the chicken is cooked through and crispy and golden on the outside, 10 to 12 minutes, flipping halfway through.

Serve the chicken tenders with the remaining honey mustard sauce for dipping.

Skinny Scoop: If you don't care for tenderloins, you can use chicken breasts and cut them into strips.

PER SERVING: **3 tenders + 2 tablespoons sauce** • CALORIES **361** • FAT **9 g** • SATURATED FAT **1.5 g** • CHOLESTEROL **126 mg** • CARBOHYDRATE **24 g** • FIBER **1 g** • PROTEIN **40 g** • SUGARS **14 g** • SODIUM **837 mg**

MY SIGNATURE WINGS

SERVES 4

20 pieces chicken wing portions (drumettes and wingettes; about 40 ounces)

¼ cup apple cider vinegar

2½ tablespoons Frank's RedHot Original sauce

1 packet (½ tablespoon) sazón seasoning with achiote (see Skinny Scoop)*

1½ teaspoons garlic powder

1 teaspoon adobo seasoning

½ teaspoon onion powder

½ teaspoon dried oregano

*Read the label to be sure this product is gluten-free.

These are my go-to wings that I've been making for years! If you follow me on Instagram Stories, you probably know we have chicken wings for dinner all the time at my house—my kids love them and they're just so easy to make. I serve them with a big salad on the side, and everyone's happy. If we're entertaining in the summer, I make a big batch of wings on the grill along with burgers, steaks, etc. The wings always disappear first, and everyone wants the recipe!

In a large bowl, toss the chicken wings with the vinegar, hot sauce, sazón, garlic powder, adobo, onion powder, and oregano. Marinate for at least 10 minutes or up to overnight in the refrigerator (the longer the better).

Remove the wings from the marinade and discard the marinade. Working in batches if needed, place the wings in the air fryer basket in a single layer. Cook at 400°F until the skin is browned and the chicken is cooked through, 22 to 25 minutes, shaking the basket halfway through. (Note: You can cook the wings in one batch if you prefer. Just add 10 to 15 minutes to the cooking time and shake the basket 3 to 4 times throughout cooking.) Serve immediately.

Skinny Scoop: Sazón is a seasoning blend sold by many brands in a variety of flavors. Look for one that has achiote (or annatto) in the ingredients list.

PER SERVING: **5 pieces** • CALORIES **340** • FAT **23 g** • SATURATED FAT **6.5 g** • CHOLESTEROL **197 mg** • CARBOHYDRATE **0 g** • FIBER **0 g** • PROTEIN **31 g** • SUGARS **0 g** • SODIUM **469 mg**

CAJUN-SPICED FRIED CHICKEN

SERVES 4

1½ tablespoons kosher salt

1 tablespoon Cajun seasoning*

1 tablespoon garlic powder

2 teaspoons sweet paprika

8 chicken drumsticks (about 3½ ounces each), skinned

1 cup buttermilk

BREADING

2/3 cup plain panko bread crumbs, wheat or gluten-free

2/3 cup crushed gluten-free cornflake crumbs

Olive oil spray

*Read the label to be sure this product is gluten-free.

These Cajun-spiced drumsticks are moist and flavorful on the inside, with a crispy golden crust on the outside. The breading is so flavorful and spicy, you honestly won't miss the skin! If your kids won't eat spicy foods, you can just omit the Cajun seasoning. This recipe is perfection—all the crispy and delicious fried chicken flavor, without all the fat you typically get from deep-frying. You can reduce the fat even more by using bone-in chicken breasts in place of drumsticks.

In a small bowl, combine the salt, Cajun seasoning, garlic powder, and paprika.

In a medium bowl, season the chicken with one-third of the spice mix (about 1 tablespoon) and toss to coat well. Pour the buttermilk over the chicken, cover, and transfer to the refrigerator to marinate for at least 6 hours or up to 12 hours. (To speed this up, you can freeze the chicken for 30 minutes, stirring halfway.)

FOR THE BREADING: In a shallow bowl, combine the panko, cornflake crumbs, and the remaining spice mix.

Remove the chicken from the buttermilk, shaking off any excess, and dredge each piece in the crumb mixture, pressing to adhere. Place the chicken on a plate.

Spritz the air fryer basket with olive oil. Working in batches if needed, place the chicken in the air fryer basket in a single layer and spritz the top of the chicken with oil. Cook at 370°F until the crumbs are golden and the chicken is cooked through, 22 to 24 minutes, flipping the chicken halfway and spritzing the tops again. Serve immediately.

PER SERVING: **2 drumsticks** · CALORIES **272** · FAT **8 g** · SATURATED FAT **2.5 g** · CHOLESTEROL **179 mg** · CARBOHYDRATE **7 g** · FIBER **0.5 g** · PROTEIN **40 g** · SUGARS **2 g** · SODIUM **885 mg**

CHICKEN CAPRESE

SERVES 4

2 boneless, skinless chicken breasts (1 pound)

¾ teaspoon kosher salt

Freshly ground black pepper

2 tablespoons mayonnaise

2 tablespoons freshly grated Parmesan cheese

2 medium vine tomatoes, thinly sliced

½ cup shredded whole milk mozzarella cheese*

Balsamic vinegar glaze (optional), for drizzling

¼ cup fresh basil leaves

*Read the label to be sure this product is gluten-free.

Originating on the island of Capri, Caprese-style salad mimics the colors of the Italian flag with its classic combination of mozzarella, tomato, and basil. Here, that combo transforms ordinary chicken cutlets into an easy and delicious meal. Chicken cutlets can be a bit boring if they're cooked without breading, but my trick of spreading a mixture of Parmesan and mayo on top adds so much flavor and makes the chicken so juicy (don't skip this step!). Serve this with steamed veggies and pasta or Israeli couscous on the side. Or opt for a big salad with some toasted bread smeared with a little pesto.

Slice the chicken breasts in half horizontally to create 4 thin cutlets. Use a mallet to pound each cutlet to a ¼-inch thickness. Season all over with the salt and pepper to taste.

In a small bowl, combine the mayonnaise and Parmesan. Spread the mixture over both sides of the chicken.

Working in batches if needed, place the chicken in the air fryer basket in a single layer. Cook at 380°F for 4 minutes. Flip the chicken and top with the tomatoes and mozzarella inside the basket. Continue to cook until the cheese has melted and the chicken is cooked through, 2 to 3 minutes more.

Transfer the chicken to a plate and drizzle with the balsamic glaze, if desired. Garnish with the basil.

PER SERVING: **1 cutlet + tomatoes and cheese** · CALORIES **250** · FAT **12 g** · SATURATED FAT **3.5 g** · CHOLESTEROL **101 mg** · CARBOHYDRATE **3 g** · FIBER **1 g** · PROTEIN **30 g** · SUGARS **2 g** · SODIUM **445 mg**

LATIN ROAST CHICKEN (POLLOCHÓN)

SERVES 4

4 garlic cloves, grated

2¼ teaspoons kosher salt

1 teaspoon freshly ground black pepper

1 teaspoon dried oregano

1 teaspoon extra-virgin olive oil

1 packet (½ tablespoon) sazón seasoning with achiote*

1 whole chicken (3½ to 4 pounds), giblets removed, patted dry with paper towels (see Skinny Scoop)

*Read the label to be sure this product is gluten-free.

Pavochón is basically a Puerto Rican-style Thanksgiving turkey—it's a whole turkey (*pavo*) that's cooked like a roast pork (*lechón*) . . . and it's unbelievably delicious! I ran with the idea and marinated a whole chicken (*pollo*) instead of a turkey. The results were wonderful: juicy on the inside and so flavorful. Achiote paste is typically used for the deep burnished color and rich flavor, but since it can be difficult to find, using sazón with achiote works perfectly. This recipe requires an air fryer basket large enough to hold a whole chicken, at least a 5.8-quart size or larger. If yours is smaller, you can use the same marinade on a cut-up chicken instead, reducing the cook time.

In a small bowl, combine the garlic, salt, pepper, and oregano to make a paste. Add the olive oil and sazón and mix well.

Using gloves to avoid staining your hands, rub the chicken inside and out with the garlic mixture. Refrigerate uncovered for at least 1 hour or up to overnight (if you don't have time to marinate it overnight, don't worry, it will still be great!). Remove the chicken from the fridge 30 to 60 minutes before you plan to cook it.

When ready to cook, place the chicken in the air fryer basket (at least a 5.8-quart size) breast side down. Cook at 350°F until the top of the chicken is browned, about 25 minutes. Flip over the chicken and continue to cook until it is crisp and browned all over and the juices run clear when you insert a knife down to the bone between the leg and the thigh, about 25 minutes more.

Transfer the chicken to a platter and let it rest for 10 minutes before carving and serving. You can serve the chicken with or without the skin depending on your preference.

Skinny Scoop: It's best to use an organic air-chilled chicken, which is fed a higher quality diet and also tastes better. Marinate overnight for best results.

PER SERVING: ¼ skinless chicken • CALORIES **177** • FAT **7.5 g** • SATURATED FAT **2 g** • CHOLESTEROL **76 mg** • CARBOHYDRATE **1 g** • FIBER **0 g** • PROTEIN **25 g** • SUGARS **0 g** • SODIUM **959 mg**

CHICKEN SATAY LETTUCE WRAPS WITH PEANUT SAUCE

SERVES 4

CHICKEN

½ cup canned light coconut milk

1½ tablespoons curry powder*

1 tablespoon fish sauce

1 tablespoon reduced-sodium soy sauce or gluten-free tamari

1 tablespoon grated fresh ginger

1 teaspoon kosher salt

6 tablespoons minced shallots

1½ pounds boneless skinless chicken breast (about 3), sliced ½-inch thick

PEANUT SAUCE

¼ cup smooth peanut butter

1½ tablespoons fresh lime juice, or more to taste

2 teaspoons reduced-sodium soy sauce or gluten-free tamari

1 teaspoon Sriracha sauce

1 teaspoon grated fresh ginger

Warm water, as needed

ASSEMBLY

Olive oil spray

1 head Boston lettuce

Lime wedges, for serving

Chopped fresh cilantro

6 tablespoons minced shallots

Tommy and I love chicken satay, a popular Indonesian dish that's typically grilled on skewers and served with a spicy peanut sauce as an appetizer. Here, I skipped the skewers and the grill and air-fried the chicken instead, which is perfect for weeknight dinners! I served the chicken and sauce wrapped in lettuce leaves garnished with lime, cilantro, and minced shallots. This would also be amazing over jasmine rice or with flatbread.

FOR THE CHICKEN: In a large bowl or zip-top plastic bag, whisk together the coconut milk, curry powder, fish sauce, soy sauce, ginger, salt, and shallots. Add the chicken and toss to completely coat. Cover and set aside for at least 30 minutes or up to 1 day in the refrigerator (the longer the better).

MEANWHILE, FOR THE PEANUT SAUCE: In a small bowl, combine the peanut butter, lime juice, soy sauce, Sriracha, and ginger and mix with a fork until smooth. Add a little bit of warm water, 1 tablespoon at a time, until it reaches a consistency loose enough to drizzle over chicken. Set aside, or refrigerate in an airtight container for up to 5 days.

TO ASSEMBLE: Spritz the air fryer basket with oil. Working in batches if needed, add the chicken to the air fryer basket in a single layer. Cook at 400°F until the chicken is cooked through in the center, 8 to 9 minutes, flipping halfway through.

Separate the head of lettuce into leaves. Serve the chicken with the lettuce leaves for wrapping and lime wedges for squeezing. Garnish with the peanut sauce, cilantro, and shallots.

*Read the label to be sure this product is gluten-free.

PER SERVING: 6 ounces chicken + 2 tablespoons sauce · CALORIES 363 · FAT 15 g · SATURATED FAT 4 g · CHOLESTEROL 124 mg · CARBOHYDRATE 13 g · FIBER 3.5 g · PROTEIN 44 g · SUGARS 6 g · SODIUM 1,049 mg

JALAPEÑO-CHEDDAR TURKEY BURGERS

SERVES 4

1 pound ground
turkey (93% lean)

¼ cup coarsely grated
cheddar cheese or nondairy
cheddar (such as Violife)

2 tablespoons plain bread
crumbs, wheat or gluten-free

1 medium jalapeño pepper,
seeded and finely minced

½ cup grated onion

1 garlic clove, grated

1 teaspoon kosher salt

⅛ teaspoon freshly
ground black pepper

Olive oil spray

4 burger buns, whole
wheat or gluten-free

4 ounces sliced avocado
(about 1 small)

Optional toppings: lettuce,
red onion, jalapeño,
sliced tomato, mayo,
ketchup, burger sauce

These juicy burgers, with jalapeños and cheese mixed right into the meat, are flavorful and delicious. They're perfect for weeknight cooking since they take less than 15 minutes to prepare and are also great for meal prep as they reheat really well. If you prefer to skip the buns, serve the burgers with lettuce wraps instead.

In a large bowl, combine the turkey, cheddar, bread crumbs, jalapeño, onion, garlic, salt, and black pepper. Mix well with your hands and then form into 4 patties ½ inch thick.

Spritz the air fryer basket with oil. Working in batches if needed, add the burgers to the air fryer basket in a single layer. Cook at 370°F until cooked through in the center and slightly browned on the outside, flipping once, 5 to 6 minutes per side.

Transfer the burgers to a plate and wipe the air fryer basket with a damp towel. Working in batches if needed, add the buns (as open halves) to the air fryer basket and cook until heated, 30 seconds.

Arrange the burgers on the buns and top with the sliced avocado and your favorite toppings. Serve immediately.

PER SERVING: **1 burger** · CALORIES **367** · FAT **18 g** · SATURATED FAT **4.5 g** · CHOLESTEROL **91 mg** · CARBOHYDRATE **24 g** · FIBER **4.5 g** · PROTEIN **30 g** · SUGARS **5 g** · SODIUM **562 mg**

ARGENTINIAN SAUSAGE SANDWICH
WITH CHIMICHURRI (CHORIPÁN)

SERVES 4

CHIMICHURRI

2 tablespoons finely chopped red onion

2 tablespoons red wine vinegar

¼ teaspoon kosher salt

2 tablespoons extra-virgin olive oil

1 garlic clove, minced

¼ cup packed fresh parsley leaves, finely chopped (no stems)

⅛ teaspoon crushed red pepper flakes, or more to taste

SANDWICHES

4 uncooked sweet Italian chicken sausage links (I like Premio), 2.8 ounces each

8 ounces whole wheat baguette or Italian bread, cut into 4 pieces

There's nothing better than a sausage sandwich, and this version, smothered in chimichurri and inspired by Argentinian *choripán*, will not disappoint! My Argentinian friends introduced me to this delicious sandwich at one of their backyard parties. It's typically grilled and served on a crusty baguette, and the sausage is usually chorizo, a mild (not smoked) pork or beef link similar to a sweet Italian sausage, seasoned with only paprika. Here, I used leaner Italian chicken sausage. What really makes this sandwich so delicious is the herby chimichurri. It's the type of sauce that makes just about everything taste better! When I make a sandwich as a main dish, I like to balance it out with a salad. A garden salad, tomato salad, or even some Savory Sweet Potato Wedges (page 167) would be a great addition here.

FOR THE CHIMICHURRI: In a medium bowl, combine the red onion, vinegar, salt, and olive oil. Let it sit for about 5 minutes to mellow out the raw onion. Add the garlic, parsley, pepper flakes, and 1 tablespoon water and whisk together.

FOR THE SANDWICHES: Preheat the air fryer to 390°F.

Place the sausages in the air fryer basket and cook until cooked through in the center, 10 to 12 minutes, flipping halfway through. Transfer to a cutting board and slice the sausages lengthwise.

Working in batches if needed, place the bread in the air fryer at 390°F for 30 seconds to warm up, then slice open. Spread 1 tablespoon chimichurri on the bottom of each bread slice, top with one sausage each and another ½ tablespoon chimichurri. Serve immediately.

PER SERVING: **1 sandwich** • CALORIES **350** • FAT **17 g** • SATURATED FAT **4 g** • CHOLESTEROL **65 mg** • CARBOHYDRATE **33 g** • FIBER **3 g** • PROTEIN **19 g** • SUGARS **4 g** • SODIUM **881 mg**

JUICY CHICKEN BREASTS

SERVES 4

4 boneless, skinless chicken breasts (about 6 ounces each)

6 cups lukewarm water

Kosher salt (see Skinny Scoop)

¾ teaspoon garlic powder

¾ teaspoon onion powder

½ teaspoon dried parsley

½ teaspoon sweet paprika

⅛ teaspoon cayenne pepper

Olive oil spray

This foolproof recipe will give you perfectly juicy chicken every time. I think it's no surprise to most of you that I prefer dark meat over white. So, if I'm cooking white breast meat, you better believe I'm adding some moisture to it! The best way to do that is to brine the breasts in a simple salt brine. (Although this may sound like a lot of sodium, only a small amount is actually absorbed.) After the brine bath, you season the chicken with lots of herbs and spices, then pop it in the fryer. The end result is versatile, juicy chicken that you can add to salads, pack for meal prep, or simply serve with a side dish.

Place the chicken breasts between two sheets of parchment and use a mallet to pound the thicker end of the chicken breasts to an even thickness on both sides so that they cook evenly.

Fill a large bowl with the water, add ¼ cup kosher salt, and stir to dissolve. Add the chicken breasts to the brine, cover, and refrigerate for 1 to 2 hours.

Remove the chicken breasts from the brine and pat dry with paper towels (discard the brine).

In a small bowl, combine ¾ teaspoon salt, the garlic powder, onion powder, parsley, paprika, and cayenne. Spritz both sides of the chicken breasts with oil and rub all over, then rub the spice mixture all over the chicken.

Working in batches if needed, add the chicken to the air fryer basket in a single layer. Cook at 380°F until the chicken is browned on the outside and cooked through, 10 to 12 minutes, flipping halfway through.

Transfer the chicken to a plate and serve immediately.

Skinny Scoop: Be sure to use Diamond Crystal brand kosher salt—any other brands or types of salt may result in salty chicken and you will have to adjust the amount.

PER SERVING: **1 breast** · CALORIES **209** · FAT **5 g** · SATURATED FAT **1 g** · CHOLESTEROL **124 mg** · CARBOHYDRATE **1 g** · FIBER **0.5 g** · PROTEIN **39 g** · SUGARS **0 g** · SODIUM **288 mg**

KOREAN-STYLE CHICKEN RICE BOWLS
WITH NAPA SLAW

SERVES 4

CHICKEN

3 boneless, skinless chicken breasts (8 ounces each)

6 tablespoons reduced-sodium soy sauce or gluten-free tamari

6 tablespoons unsweetened applesauce

6 tablespoons finely chopped yellow onion

1½ teaspoons toasted sesame oil

1½ teaspoons grated fresh ginger

1½ tablespoons light brown sugar

3 garlic cloves, grated or finely minced

1 teaspoon crushed red pepper flakes (optional)

SLAW

2 cups shredded napa cabbage

1 teaspoon toasted sesame oil

¼ cup chopped fresh cilantro

Juice of ½ lime

¼ teaspoon kosher salt

FOR SERVING

3 cups cooked brown rice

2 tablespoons prepared gochujang sauce*

½ tablespoon sesame seeds

2 scallions, thinly sliced

I used to work a few blocks away from Koreatown when I worked in NYC, and I loved going out for Korean food with my co-workers. These chicken bowls are inspired by chicken bulgogi, which I ordered all the time. The chicken breasts are juicy, sweet, spicy, and loaded with flavor. Typically, Asian pears are used in Korean marinades, but here I used applesauce since it's easier to find, and the marinade is so good you'll want to bottle it! Paired with a simple napa slaw, these rice bowls won't disappoint.

FOR THE CHICKEN: Slice the chicken breasts in half horizontally to create 6 thin cutlets. Place the cutlets between plastic wrap and pound to an even thickness, about ½ inch.

In a medium bowl, combine the soy sauce, applesauce, onion, sesame oil, ginger, brown sugar, garlic, and pepper flakes (if using). Measure out ⅓ cup of the marinade and set aside. Transfer the remaining marinade to a large zip-top plastic bag or container, add the chicken, and seal. Marinate in the refrigerator for at least 1 hour or up to overnight.

FOR THE SLAW: In a medium bowl, combine the napa cabbage, sesame oil, cilantro, lime, and salt. Set aside.

Remove the chicken from the marinade and discard the marinade. Working in batches if needed, place the chicken in the air fryer basket in a single layer. Cook at 400°F for 3 minutes. Flip the chicken, spoon the reserved ⅓ cup of marinade over the chicken, and cook until the center of the chicken is no longer pink, 3 to 4 minutes more. Transfer the chicken to a cutting board and slice.

TO SERVE: Divide the rice among four bowls and divide the chicken evenly among the portions. Top with the gochujang sauce, sesame seeds, and scallions and serve with the slaw.

*Read the label to be sure this product is gluten-free.

PER SERVING: **1 bowl** • CALORIES **439** • FAT **8.5 g** • SATURATED FAT **1.5 g** • CHOLESTEROL **124 mg** • CARBOHYDRATE **45 g** • FIBER **3.5 g** • PROTEIN **44 g** • SUGARS **9 g** • SODIUM **803 mg**

SOY-GLAZED BONELESS CHICKEN THIGHS

SERVES 4

When you think of air fryers, you typically imagine french fries or fried chicken, but this glazed chicken recipe has no breading at all. You don't need it because the air fryer does so much more as it's essentially an oven on steroids! These thighs—marinated in flavorful Asian ingredients like soy sauce, ginger, and Sriracha—come out so juicy. They're perfect over rice with steamed bok choy on the side.

¼ cup reduced-sodium soy sauce or gluten-free tamari

2½ tablespoons balsamic vinegar

1 tablespoon honey

3 garlic cloves, grated

1 teaspoon Sriracha hot sauce

1 teaspoon grated fresh ginger

8 boneless, skinless chicken thighs (4 ounces each), fat trimmed

1 scallion, green part only, sliced, for garnish

In a small bowl, combine the soy sauce, vinegar, honey, garlic, Sriracha, and ginger and mix well.

Pour half of the marinade (¼ cup) into a large bowl with the chicken and stir to coat the chicken well. Marinate in the refrigerator for at least 2 hours or up to overnight. (Reserve the remaining marinade for later.)

Remove the chicken from the marinade (discard the marinade). Working in batches if needed, transfer the chicken to the air fryer basket in a single layer. Cook at 400°F until the chicken is cooked through in the center, about 14 minutes, flipping halfway through.

Meanwhile, place the reserved ¼ cup marinade in a small pot and cook over medium-low heat for 1 to 2 minutes to reduce slightly and thicken.

To serve, drizzle the sauce over the chicken and top with the scallion.

PER SERVING: **2 thighs** · CALORIES **314** · FAT **9.5 g** · SATURATED FAT **2.5 g** · CHOLESTEROL **213 mg** · CARBOHYDRATE **9 g** · FIBER **0.5 g** · PROTEIN **46 g** · SUGARS **6 g** · SODIUM **785 mg**

KIELBASA, VEGGIE, AND PIEROGI DINNER

SERVES 4

1 medium onion, cut into 1-inch chunks

12 baby rainbow bell peppers, halved lengthwise and seeded

1 bunch (1 pound) asparagus, tough ends trimmed, cut into thirds

2 tablespoons extra-virgin olive oil

1 teaspoon chili powder

½ teaspoon garlic powder

½ teaspoon kosher salt

1 (13-ounce) package turkey kielbasa, cut on an angle into ½-inch-thick slices

12 frozen pierogies (such as Mrs. T's Classic Onion or Traditional Sauerkraut)

Whole-grain mustard, for serving (optional)

This is such an easy one-pot meal! You basically mix everything in a large bowl and then dump it right into the air fryer in two batches. Frozen pierogies are so convenient and they're loved by all in my house. I wasn't sure how they would work in the air fryer, but after playing around a bit, I found that wetting them before adding them to the fryer yields amazing results. They're plump and a little crispy on the edges, and I finish mine with some whole-grain mustard—so tasty! This is a meal in one, but you can also serve these with a green salad, a quick slaw, or a cucumber salad.

In a large bowl, combine the onion, bell peppers, asparagus, olive oil, chili powder, garlic powder, and salt and mix well. Add the kielbasa and toss to coat.

Working in batches, add half of the mixture to the air fryer basket. Cook at 400°F for 4 minutes. In a colander, wet half of the pierogi with running water for 15 seconds and add to the air fryer basket. Continue to cook, shaking the basket a few times, until the pierogies are puffy and golden brown around the edges, the sausages are browned, and the vegetables are crisp-tender, 8 to 11 minutes. Repeat with the second batch.

Transfer the kielbasa and pierogi mixture to a platter and serve with the mustard, if desired.

PER SERVING: 1⅓ cups kielbasa and veggies + 3 pierogies · CALORIES 453 · FAT 19 g · SATURATED FAT 4 g · CHOLESTEROL 61 mg · CARBOHYDRATE 49 g · FIBER 5 g · PROTEIN 22 g · SUGARS 10 g · SODIUM 1,402 mg

SAUSAGE AND PEPPER EGG ROLLS

SERVES 4

Olive oil spray

4 uncooked Italian chicken sausage links, sweet or hot (about 12 ounces)

2 medium onions, cut into ¼-inch-thick slices

2 medium red bell peppers, cut into ¼-inch-wide strips

½ teaspoon dried thyme

½ teaspoon kosher salt

Freshly ground black pepper

8 egg roll wrappers (see Skinny Scoop)

Marinara sauce (store-bought or homemade), warmed, for serving (optional)

Sausage and peppers are a staple in my home year-round because my family just loves them. Using this combo in egg rolls was actually my husband Tommy's idea, and it worked out brilliantly. The whole family went wild for these! We served them with marinara sauce and a crisp green salad on the side to make them a meal, but they would also make a great appetizer.

Spritz the air fryer basket with oil and arrange the sausages in the air fryer basket. Cook at 370°F until the sausages are browned and cooked through, about 10 minutes, flipping halfway through. Remove and transfer to a cutting board; slice the sausage very thin.

Meanwhile, in a large bowl, spritz the onions and bell peppers with oil. Season with the thyme, salt, and black pepper to taste. Arrange the onions and peppers in the air fryer basket and cook at 370°F until the vegetables are tender and slightly golden on the edges, 8 to 12 minutes, tossing the vegetables halfway through.

Working with one at a time, place an egg roll wrapper on a clean, dry surface, points facing top and bottom like a diamond. Place one-eighth of the sausages (½ sausage) and ⅓ cup of the peppers and onions just below the center of the wrapper. Fold the bottom corner over the filling and fold the left and right corners in. Lightly brush the top edges with water, then roll up tightly. Set aside and repeat with the remaining wrappers and filling.

Spritz all sides of the egg rolls with oil, using your fingers to evenly coat. Working in batches, arrange the egg rolls in the air fryer basket in a single layer. Cook at 370°F until the egg rolls are golden brown, 5 to 7 minutes, flipping halfway through.

Transfer the egg rolls to a large plate and serve immediately. If desired, serve with the marinara sauce on the side.

Skinny Scoop: Egg roll wrappers are sold in most supermarkets in the produce section near the tofu.

PER SERVING: **2 egg rolls** · CALORIES **345** · FAT **8 g** · SATURATED FAT **2 g** · CHOLESTEROL **65 mg** · CARBOHYDRATE **48 g** · FIBER **3.5 g** · PROTEIN **20 g** · SUGARS **6 g** · SODIUM **1,047 mg**

SWEDISH TURKEY MEATBALLS

SERVES 4

1 small onion, trimmed and cut crosswise into four ¼-inch-thick slices (do not separate the rings)

Olive oil spray

¼ cup plain bread crumbs, wheat or gluten-free

2¼ cups beef broth

1 large egg, lightly beaten

½ teaspoon kosher salt

¼ teaspoon freshly ground black pepper

¼ teaspoon plus ⅛ teaspoon ground allspice

¼ teaspoon plus ⅛ teaspoon ground nutmeg

1 pound ground turkey (93% lean)

2 tablespoons cornstarch

¼ teaspoon onion powder

3 tablespoons half-and-half

Chopped fresh parsley, for garnish

Leaner than beef meatballs, these tender turkey meatballs are still packed with flavor. The two-minute sauce is effortless to prepare, and although it's typically made with heavy cream, here it's thickened with cornstarch and a touch of half-and-half. Serve this over noodles, cauliflower mash, or Smashed Potatoes (page 147).

Lightly spritz the onion slices with olive oil and place in the air fryer basket. Cook at 370°F until golden, about 10 minutes. Transfer the onion to a cutting board. Discard the (dried) outer layer of the onion and finely chop the remaining slices.

In a large bowl, combine the onion, bread crumbs, ¼ cup of the beef broth, the egg, salt, black pepper, ¼ teaspoon of the allspice, and ¼ teaspoon of the nutmeg and mix well to combine.

Add the turkey and use a fork to fully combine everything (be careful not to overwork). Form the mixture into 20 meatballs 1¼ inches in diameter (about 1 ounce each).

Generously spritz the air fryer basket with olive oil. Working in batches if needed, place the meatballs in the air fryer basket in a single layer. Cook at 400°F until the meatballs are browned and cooked through, 8 to 10 minutes, flipping halfway through.

In a deep skillet, combine the remaining 2 cups broth, the cornstarch, onion powder, and the remaining ⅛ teaspoon each allspice and nutmeg. Bring to a boil over high heat, whisking until the mixture thickens, about 1 minute. Stir in the half-and-half, reduce the heat to low, and add the meatballs. Cook until the meatballs are heated through, about 1 minute.

Transfer the meatballs and sauce to a serving dish and garnish with the parsley.

PER SERVING: **5 meatballs + ⅓ cup sauce** · CALORIES **263** · FAT **12 g** · SATURATED FAT **3.5 g** · CHOLESTEROL **134 mg** · CARBOHYDRATE **12 g** · PROTEIN **27 g** · FIBER **1 g** · SUGARS **2 g** · SODIUM **593 mg**

HAWAIIAN BBQ-INSPIRED DRUMSTICKS

SERVES 4

¼ cup ketchup

¼ cup reduced-sodium soy sauce or gluten-free tamari

¼ cup unseasoned rice vinegar or apple cider vinegar

½-inch piece fresh ginger, peeled and finely grated

2 garlic cloves, finely grated

8 chicken drumsticks (2½ ounces each), skinned

2 tablespoons honey

1 teaspoon Sriracha sauce (optional)

Chopped scallions, for garnish (optional)

These drumsticks, inspired by Hawaiian huli-huli chicken, are finger-licking good! Since no grill is required, you can even make them year-round. The word *huli* means "turn" in Hawaiian, which is exactly what you should do to these drumsticks in the air fryer to prevent the marinade from burning. The marinade is similar to a teriyaki sauce, but with the addition of ketchup, an American influence. This is the type of dish the whole family will love because it has a great balance of flavors, and it's ridiculously easy to prepare—just marinate, cook, and occasionally *huli* or turn! Serve with rice or a simple potato salad and corn on the cob to make it a meal.

In a large bowl, combine the ketchup, soy sauce, vinegar, ginger, and garlic. Set aside ⅓ cup of the marinade. Add the drumsticks to the remaining marinade, cover, and refrigerate for at least 8 hours or up to overnight.

Working in batches if needed, add the drumsticks to the air fryer basket in a single layer. Cook at 400°F, flipping a few times to avoid burning, until the chicken is cooked through, about 22 minutes.

Meanwhile, add the honey and the Sriracha (if using) to the reserved ⅓ cup marinade and stir to combine.

Brush the tops of the chicken with half of the sauce and continue to cook for 30 to 60 seconds, until slightly browned. Turn the chicken, brush again with the remaining sauce, and cook 30 to 60 seconds more.

Transfer the chicken to a platter. If desired, garnish with the scallions.

PER SERVING: **2 drumsticks** · CALORIES **225** · FAT **5 g** · SATURATED FAT **1.5 g** · CHOLESTEROL **126 mg** · CARBOHYDRATE **15 g** · FIBER **0 g** · PROTEIN **29 g** · SUGARS **12 g** · SODIUM **861 mg**

FETA-BRINED STUFFED CHICKEN BREASTS

SERVES 4

4 large boneless, skinless chicken breasts (2 pounds)

4 cups feta brine (see Skinny Scoop)

Olive oil spray

1¾ teaspoons kosher salt

Freshly ground black pepper

⅔ cup crumbled feta cheese (from one 8-ounce block)

1½ cups lightly packed baby spinach, finely chopped

⅓ cup drained canned artichoke hearts, chopped

3 tablespoons chopped drained oil-packed sun-dried tomatoes

3 garlic cloves, minced or grated

Skinny Scoop: If you don't have feta brine on hand or if you need more to have enough for the total 4 cups brine called for in the recipe, you can make your own: Blend water and feta in a ratio of 1 cup water to 1 ounce (¼ cup) crumbled feta (for example, to make 4 cups brine, use 4 cups water and 4 ounces feta).

Want to know the secret to taking chicken breasts from boring to amazing? Brining! I did this with my Juicy Chicken Breasts (page 61) and the Juicy Brined Pork Chops (page 104), too. Feta cheese—the type that comes in a block, not precrumbled—is packed in a salty solution, which you can use as a brine bath. The result is an incredibly juicy and flavorful chicken that pairs perfectly with the simple pantry-driven filling of artichokes and sun-dried tomatoes. Serve the chicken with salad, wilted greens, or your favorite grain.

In a large zip-top plastic bag or medium bowl, combine the chicken breasts and the feta brine so that the chicken is submerged. Cover and marinate in the refrigerator for at least 1 hour or up to overnight (the longer the better).

Remove the chicken breasts from the brine (discard the brine). Pat the chicken dry and lightly spritz it all over with oil. Season both sides with ¼ teaspoon of the salt and black pepper to taste.

Lay the chicken breasts flat on a cutting board and cut a pocket into the thicker side of each breast, being careful not to slice all the way through the other side.

In a small bowl, combine ⅓ cup of the crumbled feta, the spinach, artichoke hearts, sun-dried tomatoes, garlic, and remaining 1½ teaspoons salt. Dividing evenly, stuff the feta mixture into the pocket of each chicken breast, and if you need to, secure the chicken around the filling with some toothpicks.

Working in batches if needed, add the chicken breasts to the air fryer basket in a single layer. Cook at 390°F for 12 minutes. Flip and top each breast with a generous tablespoon of the remaining ⅓ cup crumbled feta. Continue to cook until the chicken is completely cooked through, 7 to 8 minutes more (check for doneness by slicing partially into the center; it should no longer be pink). Serve immediately.

PER SERVING: **1 stuffed breast** · CALORIES **369** · FAT **13 g** · SATURATED FAT **5 g** · CHOLESTEROL **188 mg** · CARBOHYDRATE **5 g** · FIBER **1.5 g** · PROTEIN **56 g** · SUGARS **1 g** · SODIUM **851 mg**

Skinny Scoop: Canned water chestnuts are very mild with an incredible crunchy texture, and you can find them in most supermarkets in the Asian food section. Feel free to switch it up with canned bamboo shoots, sliced daikon radish, or even celery.

HONEY SRIRACHA CHICKEN AND VEGETABLES

SERVES 4

¼ cup honey

2 tablespoons Sriracha sauce, plus more for serving

2 tablespoons unseasoned rice vinegar

1 tablespoon soy sauce or gluten-free tamari, plus more for serving

1 teaspoon kosher salt

4 garlic cloves, minced

1¼ pounds boneless, skinless chicken thighs, cut into 1-inch pieces

1 medium yellow onion, cut into 1-inch pieces

1 red bell pepper, cut into 1-inch pieces

1 (8-ounce) can sliced water chestnuts, drained (see Skinny Scoop)

4 ounces (about 1 cup) snow peas

½ cup cashews (optional)

1 teaspoon vegetable or extra-virgin olive oil

Olive oil spray

Cooked rice, for serving (optional)

This dish is just the perfect combination of spicy and sweet—the honey in the marinade helps the chicken get deliciously browned while it cooks, and the marinade infuses this veggie-packed dinner with a ton of flavor. It's sort of like a stir-fry, only it's made in the air fryer. You'll find a delicious sauce in the bottom of the air fryer basket when this is done, but don't toss it! Instead, pour the sauce over the chicken and veggies right before serving. If you're serving this dish over rice, this dish feeds four. You can also skip the rice and make it a one-pot meal that serves two.

In a small bowl, stir together the honey, Sriracha, vinegar, soy sauce, salt, and garlic until the honey has dissolved.

In a medium bowl or zip-top plastic bag, combine the chicken with ¼ cup of the honey/Sriracha marinade. Let sit for 20 to 30 minutes at room temperature, or refrigerate for a few hours and up to overnight.

In a separate medium bowl, combine the onion, bell pepper, water chestnuts, snow peas, and cashews (if using). Add the remaining honey/Sriracha marinade and the vegetable oil and toss to coat.

Spritz the air fryer basket with oil. Add all of the chicken, along with the marinade, to the air fryer basket and cook at 370°F until the chicken is browned on the edges and cooked through in the center, 12 to 14 minutes, shaking the basket halfway through. Transfer the chicken to a plate and set aside.

Add the vegetables and their marinade to the air fryer basket all at once. Increase the air fryer temperature to 400°F and continue to cook until the vegetables are tender and browned on the edges, 10 to 15 minutes, shaking the basket halfway through. Return the chicken to the air fryer basket and cook 1 minute more, just to heat through.

If desired, serve over rice. Drizzle everything with any extra sauce from the bottom of the basket, and pass additional Sriracha and/or soy sauce at the table for drizzling.

PER SERVING: 1⅓ cups • CALORIES 324 • FAT 7 g • SATURATED FAT 1.5 g • CHOLESTEROL 133 mg • CARBOHYDRATE 34 g • FIBER 3.5 g • PROTEIN 31 g • SUGARS 24 g • SODIUM 857 mg

ONE-POT BALSAMIC CHICKEN, ASPARAGUS, AND BURST TOMATOES

SERVES 4

3 tablespoons
balsamic vinegar

2 tablespoons extra-
virgin olive oil

1 tablespoon honey

1 tablespoon Dijon mustard

3 garlic cloves, minced

12 chicken tenderloins
(1½ pounds total)

1¼ teaspoons kosher salt

½ teaspoon garlic powder

Olive oil spray

1 bunch (1 pound)
asparagus, tough ends
trimmed, cut into thirds

1 pint grape tomatoes, halved

Freshly ground black pepper

Chopped fresh basil,
for serving

This recipe was inspired by my desire to create an all-in-one meal in the air fryer similar to my sheet-pan recipes that include a protein and vegetables all cooked in the oven together, meaning just one dish to clean! After testing so many recipes for this book, I realized the bottom of the air fryer basket acts like a skillet, and the run-off liquid that accumulates beneath the tray can be used to make an easy pan sauce. For this recipe, once the chicken and veggies are cooked, transfer them to a platter, then pour all that yummy sauce over the whole dish for an easy and delicious one-pot dinner.

In a large bowl, whisk together the vinegar, oil, honey, mustard, and garlic until smooth.

Season the chicken with 1 teaspoon of the salt and the garlic powder.

Spritz the air fryer basket with oil. Working in batches if needed, place the chicken in the air fryer basket in a single layer. Cook at 400°F until browned and cooked through, about 14 minutes, flipping halfway through. Remove and transfer to the bowl with the balsamic marinade and set aside.

Add the asparagus and tomatoes to the basket in one batch and season with the remaining ¼ teaspoon salt and pepper to taste. Cook at 400°F until the asparagus is bright green and the tomatoes have started to burst, about 5 minutes, shaking the basket halfway through.

Return the chicken along with the marinade to the air fryer basket with the vegetables, mixing well so the vegetables are well coated. Cook for 2 to 3 minutes to meld the flavors, shaking the basket halfway through.

Transfer the chicken and vegetables to a serving dish and pour the balsamic marinade from the bottom of the basket all over. Garnish with the basil and serve.

PER SERVING: **3 tenderloins + 1 cup vegetables** · CALORIES **340** · FAT **12 g** · SATURATED FAT **2 g** · CHOLESTEROL **124 mg** · CARBOHYDRATE **15 g** · FIBER **3.5 g** · PROTEIN **42 g** · SUGARS **10 g** · SODIUM **534 mg**

ROASTED TURKEY BREAST

SERVES 10

1 tablespoon extra-virgin olive oil

1 bone-in, skin-on turkey breast with ribs removed (4 pounds)

2 teaspoons kosher salt

1½ teaspoons turkey or poultry seasoning

This air-fried turkey breast comes out incredibly moist and juicy, and it has a beautiful deep, golden brown skin. And big bonus, it cooks in a fraction of the time it would in the oven! I discovered this way to cook turkey a few years ago, and now it's the only way I make it when I don't want to cook a whole bird.

Rub ½ tablespoon of the oil all over the turkey breast. Season both sides with salt and turkey seasoning then rub the remaining half tablespoon of oil over the skin side.

Place the turkey in the air fryer basket skin side down. Cook at 350°F for 20 minutes. Flip and cook until a thermometer inserted into the thickest part registers 160°F, 30 to 40 minutes more depending on the size of the breast. Transfer the turkey to a cutting board, tented loosely with foil, to rest for at least 10 minutes before carving.

How to Carve a Turkey Breast
- Run a large, sharp knife along one side of the breastbone using long, even strokes. (If you are using a serrated knife, use a sawing motion.) Follow the bone all the way toward the bottom of the board.
- Bring your knife around to the front and connect where you started carving at the top of the breastbone.
- Cut down along the ribs. Follow them around and down to the bottom to connect to the bottom of the first breastbone cut. Pull the meat away from the bone and slice. Repeat the above steps on the other side of the breastbone.

PER SERVING: **4 ounces** • CALORIES **298** • FAT **14 g** • SATURATED FAT **3.5 g** • CHOLESTEROL **118 mg** • CARBOHYDRATE **0 g** • FIBER **0 g** • PROTEIN **40 g** • SUGARS **0 g** • SODIUM **331 mg**

SPICY FRIED CHICKEN CRUNCH WRAPS

SERVES 4

½ cup all-purpose flour

¼ cup cornstarch

½ cup 2% milk

4 large boneless, skinless chicken thighs (about 6 ounces each), trimmed

¾ teaspoon kosher salt

½ tablespoon light brown sugar

1 teaspoon cayenne pepper

1 teaspoon sweet paprika

½ teaspoon chili powder

½ teaspoon garlic powder

¼ teaspoon freshly ground black pepper

Olive oil spray

WRAPS

¼ cup light mayonnaise

4 teaspoons Sriracha sauce

4 (10-inch) low-carb tortillas, such as Tumaro's

1 cup shredded red cabbage

1 baby dill, thinly sliced

1 jalapeño pepper, thinly sliced

Fast-food fried chicken sandwiches are my weakness, so it doesn't get much better than this healthier unfried wrap that you can make right in your kitchen, anytime! Using tortillas in place of buns is an easy way to cut back on the calories. I opted for chicken thighs seasoned with my homemade spice mix and then wrapped it up with pickles, jalapeño, and spicy mayo.

In a shallow bowl, combine the flour and cornstarch. Place the milk in a second shallow bowl.

Season the thighs on both sides with the salt. In a small bowl, combine the brown sugar, cayenne, paprika, chili powder, garlic powder, and black pepper. Add 1½ teaspoons of the spice mix to the flour and mix well. Use the remaining seasoning on both sides of the chicken.

Dredge the chicken first in the flour mixture, then in the milk, turning to coat and shaking off any excess. Dredge the chicken one last time in the flour mixture until evenly coated, using a fork to press the chicken to adhere well. Transfer to a sheet pan or a cutting board for 10 minutes to let the coating set.

Place an air fryer parchment sheet (see page 11) in the air fryer basket and spritz it with oil. Working in batches as needed, add the chicken and spritz the tops with a bit more oil. Cook the chicken at 400°F until golden brown and the chicken is cooked through in the center, 15 to 17 minutes, flipping halfway through. Transfer to a cutting board and cut into ½-inch slices, keeping each breast together to make it easier to assemble the wraps later.

FOR THE WRAPS: In a small bowl, combine the mayo and Sriracha. Slather 1 heaping tablespoon in the center of each tortilla, top with the chicken, ¼ cup cabbage, the pickles, and jalapeño. Fold the sides over the center tightly overlapping each other to seal.

Heat a large skillet over medium heat and spritz with oil. Place the wrap, folded side down, in the skillet and cook until browned, 2 to 3 minutes per side. Cut in half and serve.

PER SERVING: 1 wrap • CALORIES 407 • FAT 13 g • SATURATED FAT 2.5 g • CHOLESTEROL 164 mg • CARBOHYDRATE 37 g • FIBER 12.5 g • PROTEIN 43 g • SUGARS 6 g • SODIUM 1,199 mg

BEEF, PORK & LAMB

CHICKEN-FRIED STEAK
WITH SAGE GRAVY

SERVES 4

This dish is classic Southern comfort food, right down to the creamy sage gravy. Chicken-fried steak is typically deep-fried in oil and served with a milk-based gravy made with the same oil the steaks were fried in. This lightened-up version, using crispy cube steak and broth for the gravy in place of oil, has less than one quarter of the fat! But it doesn't sacrifice any of the taste. In fact, Tommy asked me to keep this dish on rotation, that's how much he loved it! Make this a meal with steamed peas, broccoli, corn, or roasted carrots.

½ cup plus 1 tablespoon all-purpose flour

¼ cup cornstarch

¾ teaspoon freshly ground black pepper

1 teaspoon sweet paprika

1 cup 2% milk

1 pound lean cube steak, cut into 4 portions (see Skinny Scoop)

1 teaspoon kosher salt

1 tablespoon unsalted butter

½ cup beef or chicken broth

½ teaspoon dried sage

Olive oil spray

Preheat the oven to 200°F.

In a shallow bowl, combine ½ cup of the flour, the cornstarch, ½ teaspoon of the pepper, and the paprika. Into a separate shallow bowl, pour ½ cup of the milk.

Season the steak on both sides with the salt. Dredge the steaks first in the flour mixture, then in the milk, turning to coat and shaking off the excess. Dredge the steaks one last time in the flour mixture until evenly coated, using a fork to press them into the flour to adhere well. Transfer to a sheet pan or a cutting board for 10 minutes to let the breading set.

Meanwhile, in a medium skillet, melt the butter over medium heat and cook until foaming. When the foaming subsides, whisk in the remaining 1 tablespoon flour and continue to cook for 1 minute or so, just until the flour is blond in color and no longer smells raw.

Whisk in the broth, the remaining ½ cup milk, the remaining ¼ teaspoon black pepper, and the sage. Cook, stirring frequently, until the mixture has thickened to the consistency of gravy, 7 to 10 minutes.

Place an air fryer parchment sheet (see page 11) in the air fryer basket and spritz it with oil. Working in batches as needed, add the steak to the air fryer basket in a single layer. Spritz the top with a bit more oil and cook at 400°F until the crust is deep golden-brown, about 10 minutes, flipping halfway through. Place on a baking sheet in the preheated oven to keep warm.

Divide the steaks among plates and serve with the gravy poured on top. The gravy thickens a lot as it cools, so if needed, gently warm over medium-low heat to thin it out before serving.

Skinny Scoop: Cube steak has been pounded (tenderized) already by the butcher. If you can't find it, or if you'd prefer, use 4-ounce sirloin steaks and pound them to a ¼-inch thickness.

PER SERVING: **1 steak + 2½ tablespoons gravy** · CALORIES **267** · FAT **9 g** · SATURATED FAT **4.5 g** · CHOLESTEROL **81 mg** · CARBOHYDRATE **16 g** · FIBER **0.5 g** · PROTEIN **29 g** · SUGARS **3 g** · SODIUM **436 mg**

SPICE-RUBBED LAMB CHOPS
WITH CUCUMBERS AND YOGURT

SERVES 4

1 teaspoon kosher salt

¼ teaspoon ground cumin

½ teaspoon sweet paprika

¼ teaspoon chili powder*

8 lamb loin chops (about 3½ ounces each), fat trimmed

SALAD

1 English cucumber, sliced

1 teaspoon fresh lemon juice

1 teaspoon red wine vinegar

½ tablespoon extra-virgin olive oil

¼ teaspoon kosher salt

Freshly ground black pepper

FOR SERVING

1 cup 2% Greek yogurt

½ teaspoon grated lemon zest

2 tablespoons chopped fresh mint

Crushed red pepper flakes

Lemon wedges

*Read the label to be sure this product is gluten-free.

Lamb loin chops are my go-to for weeknights when I need a quick and tasty meal. They're leaner than lamb rib chops and they resemble mini T-bone steaks. When the weather is warm, I usually grill them, but the beauty of making them in the air fryer is that you can make them year-round. Fresh cucumbers and mint complement the spices, and you can serve it with a side of couscous to make it a meal.

In a small bowl, combine the salt, cumin, paprika, and chili powder. Rub the mixture all over the lamb chops.

Working in batches if needed, place the lamb in the air fryer basket in a single layer. Cook at 400°F until a thermometer inserted in the side of each chop registers 145°F for medium-rare (or longer to your taste), flipping once, about 4 minutes per side.

FOR THE SALAD: In a medium bowl, toss the cucumber with the lemon juice, vinegar, oil, salt, and pepper to taste.

TO SERVE: Spoon ¼ cup of the yogurt onto each of four plates and top each with one-quarter of the cucumber salad. Place 2 lamb chops on each plate and top everything with the lemon zest and mint. Sprinkle with pepper flakes to taste and serve with the lemon wedges alongside.

PER SERVING: **2 chops (4 ounces meat, without bone) + salad** · CALORIES **334** · FAT **13 g** · SATURATED FAT **5 g** · CHOLESTEROL **134 mg** · CARBOHYDRATE **6 g** · FIBER **0.5 g** · PROTEIN **47 g** · SUGARS **3 g** · SODIUM **503 mg**

BEEF TATAKI
WITH GINGER-LEMON DRESSING

SERVES 4

1 sirloin steak (20 ounces),
at least 1 inch thick
(see Skinny Scoop)

1 teaspoon kosher salt

¼ teaspoon freshly
ground black pepper

SAUCE

¼ cup fresh lemon juice

2 tablespoons reduced-sodium
soy sauce or gluten-free tamari

1 tablespoon mirin

1 teaspoon grated fresh ginger

FOR SERVING

4 cups loosely packed arugula

5 scallions, thinly sliced
(about ½ cup)

1 teaspoon toasted
sesame seeds

Tataki is a popular Japanese method for preparing beef, in which the meat is lightly seared over high heat, leaving the center pink. To get the steaks pink and tender on the inside but browned and evenly cooked on the outside while using the air fryer, be sure to look for steaks that are at least 1 inch thick. Once cooked, the steaks are thinly sliced and served over a bed of arugula with an easy and delicious lemon and ginger-infused soy sauce. This is perfect all on its own, or you can serve it with rice if you want to include a grain.

Pat the steaks dry and season with the salt and pepper.

Preheat the air fryer to 400°F for 3 to 5 minutes.

Add the steak to the air fryer basket and cook for 5 minutes. Flip and continue to cook until a thermometer inserted into the thickest part of the steak registers 130°F for medium-rare, 3 to 5 minutes more, depending on the thickness.

Transfer the steak to a cutting board and let rest for 10 minutes before slicing very thinly.

MEANWHILE, FOR THE SAUCE: In a small bowl, whisk together all of the ingredients until smooth.

TO SERVE: Place the arugula on a large platter and arrange the sliced steak on top. Drizzle with half of the sauce, then top with the scallions and the sesame seeds. Serve with the remaining sauce at the table, for dipping.

Skinny Scoop: Look for steaks with as even a thickness as possible. If your air fryer is small, you can cut the steak in half and cook this in two batches.

PER SERVING: **4 ounces steak + 1 cup salad plus dressing** · CALORIES **221** · FAT **8 g** · SATURATED FAT **2.5 g** · CHOLESTEROL **95 mg** · CARBOHYDRATE **6 g** · FIBER **1 g** · PROTEIN **32 g** · SUGARS **3 g** · SODIUM **669 mg**

PROSCIUTTO-WRAPPED PORK TENDERLOIN
WITH FIG-MUSTARD SAUCE

SERVES 4

1 pork tenderloin
(about 1 pound)

Freshly ground black pepper

5 thin strips prosciutto
(2½ ounces total)

2 tablespoons fig preserves

4 teaspoons whole-
grain mustard

2 teaspoons white
wine vinegar

This pork dish, made with only six ingredients, is incredibly easy to prepare. The salty-sweet combo of the fig preserves and the prosciutto is really lovely. No searing or strings to tie the tenderloin are needed; simply wrap it and cook! If your air fryer basket is on the small side, cutting the tenderloin in half works best.

Season the tenderloin with black pepper to taste. Wrap the prosciutto around the tenderloin so each strip is touching and just slightly overlapping.

If needed, cut the tenderloin in half to fit into the air fryer basket. Place the tenderloin in the air fryer basket and cook at 400°F for 10 minutes. Flip the tenderloin and continue to cook until an instant-read thermometer inserted into the center reads 145° to 150°F, 6 to 10 minutes more (this will depend on the thickness of the tenderloin, so start checking after 5 minutes). Transfer the tenderloin to a plate and let rest about 5 minutes.

Meanwhile, in a small bowl, whisk together the fig preserves, mustard, and vinegar.

Slice the pork into 8 slices, drizzle with the fig sauce, and serve.

PER SERVING: **2 slices pork + about 1 tablespoon sauce** · CALORIES **194** · FAT **4 g** · SATURATED FAT **1.5 g** · CHOLESTEROL **86 mg** · CARBOHYDRATE **8 g** · FIBER **0 g** · PROTEIN **29 g** · SUGARS **7 g** · SODIUM **638 mg**

STEAK, POTATO, AND POBLANO BURRITOS

SERVES 4

STEAK

1 sirloin steak (12 ounces)

½ teaspoon kosher salt

½ teaspoon garlic powder

¾ teaspoon ground cumin

Olive oil spray

GUACAMOLE

4 ounces avocado
(about 1 small)

2 tablespoons diced red onion

Juice of ½ lime

Pinch of kosher salt

POTATOES

1 medium (12-ounce) russet
potato, cut into ½-inch cubes

1 poblano pepper, seeded
and cut into ½-inch pieces

1½ tablespoons extra-
virgin olive oil

½ teaspoon kosher salt

Freshly ground black pepper

Olive oil spray

FOR ASSEMBLY

4 (8-inch) tortillas, low-carb
whole wheat or gluten-free

½ cup shredded Mexican
cheese blend*

These burritos are ideal for the meat-and-potato lovers in your home! Filled with spice-rubbed sirloin steak, potatoes, cheese, and guacamole, all wrapped up in a tortilla, they come together really quickly. Serve them with sour cream, salsa, or your favorite hot sauce, if you'd like.

FOR THE STEAK: Season the steak with the salt, garlic powder, and cumin.

FOR THE GUACAMOLE: In a medium bowl, combine the avocado, red onion, lime juice, and salt. Mash with a fork until combined but still slightly chunky. Cover and set aside.

Preheat the air fryer to 400°F.

Spritz the basket with oil. Add the steak to the air fryer basket and cook, flipping halfway, until medium-rare, 10 to 15 minutes (depending on the thickness). Transfer the steak to a cutting board, tent with foil, and let rest while making the potatoes.

FOR THE POTATOES: Wipe the air fryer basket clean. In a medium bowl, combine the potatoes, poblano, olive oil, salt, and black pepper to taste. Reduce the air fryer temperature to 350°F and spritz the basket with oil. Add the potatoes to the basket and cook until golden, about 15 minutes, flipping with a spatula halfway through.

TO ASSEMBLE: Warm the tortillas directly over a gas stove flame or in a skillet until warmed through.

Slice the steak across the grain into very thin slices, then cut the slices into small bite-size pieces. On a clean work surface, working with one tortilla at a time, layer one-quarter of the steak, potatoes, guacamole, and cheese blend in the middle of the tortilla. Lift the edge nearest you and wrap it around the filling. Fold in the left and right sides toward the center and continue to roll into a tight cylinder. Set aside, seam side down, and repeat with the remaining tortillas and filling. Serve immediately.

*Read the label to be sure this product is gluten-free.

PER SERVING: 1 burrito · CALORIES 410 · FAT 20 g · SATURATED FAT 5 g · CHOLESTEROL 64 mg · CARBOHYDRATE 37 g · FIBER 17 g · PROTEIN 32 g · SUGARS 3 g · SODIUM 760 mg

CHEESEBURGER-LOADED FRIES

SERVES 2

CHEESEBURGER

½ pound ground beef (93% lean)

2 tablespoons reduced-fat shredded cheddar cheese*

½ tablespoon yellow mustard

½ teaspoon kosher salt

¼ teaspoon onion powder

SPECIAL SAUCE

2 tablespoons light mayonnaise

2 teaspoons ketchup

½ teaspoon yellow mustard

½ teaspoon dill pickle juice

⅛ teaspoon onion powder

⅛ teaspoon garlic powder

⅛ teaspoon sweet paprika

FRIES

2 medium potatoes (12 ounces)

2 teaspoons olive oil

¼ teaspoon kosher salt

¼ teaspoon garlic powder

Freshly ground black pepper

Olive oil spray

TOPPINGS

¼ cup chopped lettuce

1 small diced tomato

¼ cup chopped red onion

¼ cup chopped dill pickle

I know you've had french fries with your burger, but have you ever put french fries ON your burger!? I've been doing that since my high school cafeteria days, and I still do it today. Here, I flipped this combo by topping fries with chopped cheeseburger and other delicious burger toppings. To streamline this recipe further, use frozen fries.

Preheat the oven to 200°F.

FOR THE CHEESEBURGER: In a large bowl, combine the beef, cheddar, mustard, salt, and onion powder and mix until well combined. Gently form the meat mixture into 2 equal patties and flatten each one slightly to about a ⅓-inch thickness. Use your finger to press down into the center of each patty to create a dimple, which will prevent too much shrinking.

FOR THE SPECIAL SAUCE: In a medium bowl, stir all of the ingredients until smooth.

Arrange the burgers in the air fryer basket and cook at 400°F to medium doneness, about 10 minutes, flipping halfway through. Place on a sheet pan, cover with foil, and transfer to the oven to keep warm.

FOR THE FRIES: Wash and dry the potatoes. Cut them lengthwise into ¼-inch-thick slices; then cut each slice into ¼-inch-thick fries. (A mandoline is helpful here.)

In a bowl, toss the potatoes with the olive oil. Season with the salt, garlic powder, and black pepper to taste and toss to coat.

Working in 2 batches, spritz the air fryer basket with oil. Add half of the potatoes to the basket in an even layer, without overlapping or crowding. Cook at 380°F until the potatoes are golden and crisp, 12 to 14 minutes, flipping halfway through.

To serve, divide the potatoes between two plates. Chop the burger patties into small bite-size pieces and scatter on top of the fries. Drizzle everything with the special sauce, top with the lettuce, tomatoes, onions, and pickles. Serve immediately.

*Read the label to be sure this product is gluten-free.

PER SERVING: 2¼ cups • CALORIES 416 • FAT 18 g • SATURATED FAT 5.5 g • CHOLESTEROL 78 mg • CARBOHYDRATE 35 g • FIBER 5.5 g • SUGARS 6 g • PROTEIN 30 g • SODIUM 966 mg

ROSEMARY FLANK STEAK
WITH PANKO ONION RINGS

SERVES 4

BUTTERMILK BATTER

2/3 cup light buttermilk

1 large egg

1/4 cup unbleached
all-purpose flour

1 teaspoon Lawry's Seasoned
Salt or your favorite brand

STEAK

2 teaspoons chopped
fresh rosemary

2 large garlic cloves, grated or
crushed through a garlic press

2 teaspoons extra-
virgin olive oil

1 1/4 pounds flank steak

1 teaspoon kosher salt

ONION RINGS

2 cups panko bread crumbs

1/2 teaspoon Lawry's
Seasoned Salt or your
favorite brand

Olive oil spray

16 (3/4-inch) slices Vidalia
onion (from 2 large onions
2 1/2 to 3 inches in diameter)

Skinny Scoop: Chilling the
buttermilk batter helps it adhere
to the smooth surface of the
onion rings.

We're steak lovers in my house, and Tommy loves a good onion ring, so this meal was definitely family-approved! Flank steak, a lean cut of beef that is super flavorful, benefits from quick, high-heat cooking, making it perfect for the air fryer. Marinating it for at least 30 minutes before cooking is ideal for tender and tasty results.

FOR THE BUTTERMILK BATTER: In a medium bowl, whisk together the buttermilk, egg, flour, and seasoned salt. Cover and chill in the refrigerator for 30 minutes (see Skinny Scoop).

FOR THE STEAK: In a small bowl, combine the rosemary, garlic, and olive oil to make a loose paste. On a large plate, slather the steak with the mixture and season with the salt.

Preheat the oven to 250°F.

FOR THE ONION RINGS: Place the panko in a shallow dish with the seasoned salt. Remove the batter from the refrigerator.

Lightly spritz the air fryer basket with oil. Working in batches, use a fork to dip each onion ring into the buttermilk mixture, then into the panko, turning to coat. Lift out each ring with a fork, gently shake off any excess crumbs, and place in the air fryer basket in an even layer, leaving about 1/2 inch between the rings. Spritz both sides of the rings with oil. Cook at 340°F until crisp and lightly browned, 10 to 12 minutes, flipping halfway through. Transfer to a baking sheet and place in the oven to keep warm.

If needed, cut the steak in half across the grain to fit in the air fryer. Working in batches if needed, add the steak to the air fryer and cook at 400°F until a thermometer inserted into the thickest part registers 130°F for medium-rare, 14 to 15 minutes, flipping halfway throughy. (The timing will depend on the thickness of the steak.) Transfer the steak to a cutting board, tent with foil, and let rest for 5 minutes.

Slice the steak thinly across the grain. Divide the steak and the onion rings among plates to serve.

PER SERVING: **4 ounces steak + 4 onion rings** • CALORIES **385** • FAT **12 g** • SATURATED FAT **4.5 g** • CHOLESTEROL **122 mg** • CARBOHYDRATE **31 g** • FIBER **2.5 g** • PROTEIN **36 g** • SUGARS **11 g** • SODIUM **752 mg**

PORK MILANESE
WITH TRICOLORE SALAD

SERVES 4

When we go out for Italian, I usually order the veal Milanese as it's my absolute favorite. But I rarely cook veal at home. Instead, I make the classic dish with thin sliced pork loin, which come out crisp and delicious in the air fryer. The pork pairs wonderfully with this colorful, lemony salad of mixed bitter greens. Most recipes in the air fryer don't require preheating, but I find it helps with thin cutlets because the actual cook time is so short.

PORK

8 thin slices pork loin (about 3 ounces each), trimmed of excess fat

¾ teaspoon kosher salt

1 cup seasoned bread crumbs, wheat or gluten-free

¼ cup freshly grated Parmesan cheese

2 large eggs

Olive oil spray

SALAD

2 cups baby arugula

½ small head radicchio, chopped (about 2 cups)

1 endive, sliced crosswise

2 tablespoons fresh lemon juice

1 tablespoon extra-virgin olive oil

½ teaspoon kosher salt

Freshly ground black pepper, to taste

2 lemons, cut into wedges, for serving

FOR THE PORK: Place the pork slices between 2 sheets of plastic wrap on a flat surface. With a meat pounder or a mallet, pound them to a ¼-inch thickness. Season the cutlets on both sides with the salt.

In a shallow bowl, combine the bread crumbs and Parmesan. In a separate shallow bowl, beat the eggs with 1 tablespoon water. Working in batches, dip the cutlets in the egg mixture, shake to remove any excess, then dip them into the bread crumb mixture and press to coat.

Transfer the cutlets to a large plate or cutting board and spritz both sides generously with oil.

Preheat the air fryer to 400°F.

Working in batches, place the pork in the air fryer basket in a single layer. Cook until the crumbs are golden-brown and the meat is cooked through, 6 to 7 minutes, flipping halfway through.

MEANWHILE, FOR THE SALAD: In a large bowl, combine all the salad ingredients and toss to coat.

To serve, arrange 2 cutlets on each plate along with 1 cup salad and the lemon wedges.

PER SERVING: **2 cutlets + 1 cup salad** • CALORIES **374** • FAT **13 g** • SATURATED FAT **3.5 g** • CHOLESTEROL **146 mg** • CARBOHYDRATE **19 g** • FIBER **2.5 g** • PROTEIN **47 g** • SUGARS **3 g** • SODIUM **1,078 mg**

GOUDA-STUFFED BEEF AND MUSHROOM BURGERS

SERVES 4

8 ounces sliced cremini (baby bella) mushrooms

1 teaspoon extra-virgin olive oil

1 tablespoon balsamic vinegar

1 pound ground beef (93% lean)

1 teaspoon kosher salt

¾ teaspoon freshly ground black pepper

¾ teaspoon onion powder

½ teaspoon garlic powder

¼ teaspoon dried thyme

2 ounces Gouda cheese, cut into ¼-inch dice

2 tablespoons diced pickles, plus 8 pickle chips for topping

4 low-calorie hamburger buns, whole wheat or gluten-free

4 lettuce leaves

8 slices tomato (from 1 large)

Blending mushrooms with lean ground beef gives these burgers an earthy flavor and an extra boost of vitamin D, allowing you to enjoy a super-size burger without the extra calories. Gouda is a mild cheese and it melts nicely tucked inside the burger patty. For a tangier twist, try adding Roquefort, which also pairs well with mushrooms. If you can't find creminis, white button mushrooms work just as well. Serve the patties on a bun with all the fixin's, or skip the bun and turn the burgers into lettuce wraps for a low-carb meal.

In a medium bowl, combine the mushrooms, oil, and vinegar and toss to coat the mushrooms well. Working in batches if needed, place the mushrooms in the air fryer basket in a single layer. Cook at 380°F until tender, about 5 minutes, shaking the basket halfway through. Transfer the mushrooms to a cutting board and let cool before finely chopping them.

In a large bowl, combine the chopped mushrooms, beef, salt, pepper, onion powder, garlic powder, and thyme and mix gently. Divide the beef/mushroom mixture evenly into 4 portions and gently shape each into a ball. Use your finger to press a well into the center of each ball and add one-quarter of the Gouda and ½ tablespoon of the diced pickles to each well. Close the well to seal the cheese and pickles inside. Press each ball into a patty about 3½ inches in diameter and about ¾ inch thick.

Working in batches if needed, place the patties in the air fryer basket in a single layer. Cook at 370°F until the burgers are cooked to medium doneness and the cheese is melted, 9 to 11 minutes, flipping halfway through.

Serve the burgers on the buns and top with the lettuce, tomato, pickles, and your favorite condiments.

PER SERVING: **1 burger** · CALORIES **363** · FAT **15 g** · SATURATED FAT **6 g** · CHOLESTEROL **88 mg** · CARBOHYDRATE **22 g** · FIBER **3.5 g** · PROTEIN **36 g** · SUGARS **7 g** · SODIUM **728 mg**

JUICY BRINED PORK CHOPS

SERVES 4

¼ cup kosher salt

4 cups lukewarm water

4 bone-in center-cut pork chops (6½ ounces each, ¾ to 1 inch thick), trimmed of fat

Olive oil spray

DRY RUB

2 teaspoons sweet paprika

1 teaspoon garlic powder

1 teaspoon onion powder

½ teaspoon dried thyme

½ teaspoon dried sage

¼ teaspoon freshly ground black pepper

You can seriously up your pork chop game by brining them, and it's so easy. A little brining and a flavorful dry rub go a long way to making the perfect pork chop—tender and juicy. Brine them in the morning and they will be ready for cooking at dinnertime! Pork chops can be brined anywhere from 8 to 12 hours in the refrigerator, but if they're brined any longer, the meat will taste too salty. Also, an instant-read thermometer is a must to ensure your chops are cooked to just the right doneness; I like to cook mine to an internal temp of 145°F.

In a large bowl, dissolve the salt in the water. Add the pork chops to the brine, cover, and refrigerate for at least 8 hours or up to 12 hours.

Remove the chops from the brine, rinse, and pat dry with paper towels (discard the brine). Spritz both sides of the pork chops with oil.

FOR THE DRY RUB: In a small bowl, combine all the ingredients. Coat the pork chops all over with the dry rub.

Spritz the air fryer basket with oil. Working in batches if needed, add the pork chops to the air fryer basket in a single layer. Cook at 400°F until a thermometer inserted into the thickest part registers 145°F, 12 to 15 minutes, flipping halfway through.

Transfer the pork chops to a platter and let stand for 5 minutes before serving.

PER SERVING: 1 chop · CALORIES **243** · FAT **7 g** · SATURATED FAT **2 g** · CHOLESTEROL **127 mg** · CARBOHYDRATE **2 g** · FIBER **0.5 g** · PROTEIN **41 g** · SUGARS **0 g** · SODIUM **144 mg**

BEEF AND BROCCOLI

SERVES 4

GF DF

Yes, you can make this Chinese take-out staple in an air fryer! This recipe shows the different cooking methods at your disposal with the air fryer: First, you use it to steam-roast the broccoli, which results in lightly browned edges while retaining the vegetable's snap. Then, at a higher temperature, you "sear" tender strips of steak marinated in a savory, zingy sauce. You use that same marinade to make a quick stovetop sauce—you'll want a spoon to finish every last drop!

1 pound flank steak

1/2 cup reduced-sodium soy sauce or gluten-free tamari

1/4 cup water or low-sodium chicken broth

1 tablespoon light brown sugar

4 garlic cloves, minced

1-inch piece fresh ginger, minced or grated

1/2 teaspoon crushed red pepper flakes (optional)

1 pound broccoli florets (from 1 large head), cut into bite-size pieces

1 tablespoon toasted sesame oil

2 teaspoons cornstarch

1/2 tablespoon toasted sesame seeds, for garnish

Slice the beef across the grain into strips about 1/4 inch thick (this is easier if you freeze the beef for 15 to 20 minutes first). Slice the strips into thirds.

In a large bowl, whisk together the soy sauce, water, brown sugar, garlic, ginger, and pepper flakes (if using). Add the steak and toss to coat. Set aside to marinate for at least 20 to 30 minutes at room temperature or up to overnight in the fridge.

In a large bowl, combine the broccoli, sesame oil, and 1 tablespoon water and toss to lightly coat.

Working in batches if needed, place the broccoli in the air fryer basket so that it comes to about one-third to halfway up the sides. Cook at 370°F until the broccoli is tender and browned along some edges but still crisp, 6 to 8 minutes, shaking the basket halfway through. Remove and set aside in the same large bowl.

Pour the marinade from the beef into a large skillet and set aside.

Working in batches if needed, arrange half of the beef in the air fryer basket in a single layer. Cook at 400°F just until the outside is browned and the edges are starting to crisp up, 3 to 4 minutes, flipping with tongs halfway through. Transfer the beef to the bowl with the broccoli, and pour any sauce that accumulated in the bottom of the air fryer basket over the bowl as well. Repeat with the remaining beef.

In a small bowl or cup, combine the cornstarch with 1 tablespoon water and mix until dissolved. Whisk the cornstarch mixture into the marinade in the skillet and bring to a simmer over medium heat. Cook, stirring occasionally, just until the sauce thickens a bit, 1 to 2 minutes. Add the beef and broccoli and toss to coat.

To serve, divide the beef and broccoli among four plates and garnish with the sesame seeds.

PER SERVING: 1 1/4 cups · CALORIES 284 · FAT 12 g · SATURATED FAT 3.5 g · CHOLESTEROL 78 mg · CARBOHYDRATE 16 g · FIBER 3.5 g · PROTEIN 30 g · SUGARS 6 g · SODIUM 1,167 mg

LAMB LOIN CHOPS
WITH PISTACHIO-MINT GREMOLATA

SERVES 4

8 bone-in lamb loin chops
(4 ounces each, 1 inch thick),
trimmed of excess fat

Kosher salt and freshly
ground black pepper

½ teaspoon ground cinnamon

Olive oil spray

GREMOLATA

1 cup packed baby
arugula, finely chopped

¼ cup finely chopped
fresh mint

¼ cup salted roasted
pistachios, chopped

1 medium garlic clove, minced

Grated zest of 1 lemon,
plus 2 teaspoons juice

¼ teaspoon kosher salt

¼ teaspoon freshly
ground black pepper

These lamb loin chops require minimal effort, but the payoff is huge. They're simply rubbed with just enough cinnamon and black pepper to add earthiness to the already flavorful meat. For a fresh contrast to the rich lamb, the dish is finished with a lively gremolata that's full of mint, pistachios, and a peppery punch from the arugula. For best results, the chops should be about 1 inch thick, which will ensure that they will caramelize and brown beautifully, but also cook evenly through to the perfect temperature.

Sprinkle the lamb chops with ¾ teaspoon salt, ½ teaspoon pepper, and the cinnamon. Spritz the chops with olive oil.

Spritz the air fryer basket with oil. Working in batches if needed, place the chops in the air fryer basket in a single layer. Cook at 400°F until a thermometer inserted into the lamb registers 145°F for medium-rare, 8 to 10 minutes, flipping halfway through (or longer for medium).

Meanwhile, **FOR THE GREMOLATA:** In a small bowl, combine all the gremolata ingredients.

Serve the chops topped with the gremolata.

PER SERVING: **2 lamb chops + 3 tablespoons gremolata** · CALORIES **374** · FAT **19 g** · SATURATED FAT **6.5 g** · CHOLESTEROL **150 mg** · CARBOHYDRATE **4 g** · FIBER **1.5 g** · PROTEIN **47 g** · SUGARS **1 g** · SODIUM **481 mg**

STEAK FAJITAS

SERVES 4

1 (1-pound) sirloin steak, at least 1 inch thick

Kosher salt

2 teaspoons ground cumin

1 teaspoon garlic powder

2 medium onions, sliced into ¼-inch-wide strips

2 medium bell peppers (use a mix of colors), cut into ¼-inch-wide strips

1 tablespoon extra-virgin olive oil

4 ounces avocado (about 1 small)

Juice of ½ lime

Olive oil spray

8 corn tortillas, warmed

½ cup reduced-fat shredded Mexican cheese blend* or nondairy alternative

Sour cream, for serving (optional)

*Read the label to be sure this product is gluten-free.

My husband, Tommy, loves fajitas, so they're on the menu in my house at least once a month. In the summer we grill them, but I was impressed with how well they turned out in the air fryer. Air-frying the steak is so easy, and I love that there's no splatter on the stove since the mess is all contained in the air fryer! This recipe comes together fast, and it is sure to please all the Mexican food lovers in your house.

Pat the steak dry and season all over with 1 teaspoon salt, the cumin, and garlic powder.

In a large bowl, combine the onions, bell peppers, olive oil, and ¼ teaspoon salt. In a small bowl, combine the avocado, lime juice, and ¼ teaspoon salt and mash with a fork until mostly smooth.

Preheat the air fryer to 400°F for 3 to 5 minutes.

Spritz the basket with oil, add the steak, and spritz the top with oil. Cook for 5 minutes, then flip. Continue cooking until a thermometer inserted into the thickest part registers 130° to 135°F for medium to medium-rare, another 3 to 4 minutes, depending on the thickness.

Transfer the steak to a plate and let rest while the vegetables cook.

Place the onions and peppers in the air fryer basket in one batch. Reduce the air fryer temperature to 350°F. Cook until the vegetables are tender, about 12 minutes, shaking the basket halfway through.

Cut the steak into ¼-inch-thick slices and add to the vegetables in the air fryer along with any pan juices from the plate. Cook to heat 30 to 60 seconds.

To assemble, evenly distribute the steak and vegetables (about ½ cup per tortilla) among the 8 tortillas. Top with the guacamole, cheese, and sour cream (if using).

PER SERVING: **2 fajitas** · CALORIES **416** · FAT **17 g** · SATURATED FAT **4.5 g** · CHOLESTEROL **77 mg** · CARBOHYDRATE **35 g** · FIBER **7.5 g** · PROTEIN **33 g** · SUGARS **6 g** · SODIUM **623 mg**

SEAFOOD

MUSTARD-DILL SALMON
WITH ASPARAGUS

SERVES 2

2 wild salmon fillets (about 6 ounces each), skinned

½ lemon, cut into 2 wedges

⅛ teaspoon kosher salt

1½ tablespoons mayonnaise (I like Sir Kensington's)

½ tablespoon Dijon mustard

1 tablespoon minced fresh dill, plus more for garnish

Olive oil spray

1 bunch asparagus (1 pound), tough ends trimmed

Capers, for garnish (optional)

Salmon is my favorite protein to make in the air fryer. It's super quick, always comes out perfectly cooked, and it doesn't stink up the whole kitchen! To make this a meal, I steam some asparagus for 2 to 3 minutes in the microwave while the salmon cooks. The whole meal is ready in under 15 minutes from start to finish.

Season the salmon with the juice of 1 lemon wedge and the salt.

In a small bowl, combine the mayonnaise, mustard, and dill. Spread over the top of the salmon.

Preheat the air fryer to 400°F.

Spritz the basket with olive oil. Place the salmon fillets in the air fryer basket. Cook until the fish flakes easily with a fork, 7 to 8 minutes, or longer depending on the thickness of the salmon.

Meanwhile, place the asparagus in a microwave-safe dish with 1 tablespoon water. Partially cover and cook until tender-crisp, 2 to 3 minutes, depending on the thickness of the spears. Squeeze the remaining lemon wedge over the asparagus.

Garnish the fish with dill and top with the capers (if using). Serve with the asparagus.

PER SERVING: **1 salmon fillet + ½ bunch asparagus spears** · CALORIES **372** · FAT **19 g** · SATURATED FAT **2.5 g** · CHOLESTEROL **101 mg** · CARBOHYDRATE **10 g** · FIBER **5 g** · PROTEIN **39 g** · SUGARS **5 g** · SODIUM **319 mg**

KING CRAB LEGS
WITH GARLIC-LEMON BUTTER

SERVES 4

2 pounds frozen king, snow, or Dungeness crab legs, rinsed

4 tablespoons unsalted butter or nondairy butter

1 garlic clove, minced

Juice of 1/2 lemon, plus 1 lemon, cut into wedges, for serving

In the air fryer, king crab legs go from freezer to table in under 20 minutes! I always have crab legs in my freezer because they're so easy to whip up for last-minute appetizers or dinner. They're already cooked, so all you're really doing is heating them up. Curiosity pushed me to try them in the air fryer instead of boiling them, and I'm so glad I did! It's so fast, you don't even have to boil a pot of water. Just pop them into the air fryer, easy as that. Serve with corn on the cob, salad, or Smashed Potatoes (page 147).

If needed, cut the crab legs so they fit in the air fryer basket. Working in batches if needed, cook at 300°F until heated through, about 15 minutes, flipping halfway through. (Smaller legs may take less time.)

Meanwhile, in a small pot, melt the butter over medium-low heat. Reduce the heat to low, add the garlic, and simmer until fragrant but not browned, 4 to 5 minutes. Remove from the heat and add the lemon juice.

Divide the garlic-lemon butter among four small bowls and serve alongside the crab legs for dipping and the lemon wedges for squeezing over the crab.

PER SERVING: 1/2 pound legs + 1 tablespoon butter · CALORIES 356 · FAT 14 g · SATURATED FAT 7.5 g · CHOLESTEROL 203 mg · CARBOHYDRATE 4 g · FIBER 0 g · PROTEIN 51 g · SUGARS 0.5 g · SODIUM 859 mg

SESAME-CRUSTED TUNA
WITH WASABI MAYO

SERVES 4

2 tablespoons black sesame seeds

2 tablespoons white sesame seeds

4 tuna steaks (6 ounces each, 1½ inches thick)

2 teaspoons toasted sesame oil

¼ teaspoon kosher salt

Freshly ground black pepper

¼ cup light mayonnaise

½ tablespoon wasabi paste

1 lemon, cut into wedges

4 cups baby arugula

This dish looks fancy, but it couldn't be simpler and takes less than 15 minutes from start to finish. I'm so lucky that my neighbor, an avid fisherman, shares his fresh summer tuna catch with me, but when you buy tuna from a seafood counter or fish market, be sure to look for a firm texture and rich, red color. If you want to serve this with a grain, brown or black rice would be great. The cook time will vary slightly depending on the thickness of the tuna steaks. Since the fish cooks so fast, it's best to get tuna steaks around 1½ inches thick to keep the center rare.

Combine the black and white sesame seeds on a small plate. Lightly coat the tuna steaks with the sesame oil and season both sides with the salt and pepper to taste.

Preheat the air fryer to 400°F.

Press each tuna steak into the sesame seed mixture until both sides are thoroughly and evenly coated. (It's helpful to use tongs to hold the tuna by the sides for this.)

Working in batches, arrange the tuna in the air fryer basket in a single layer. Cook until the seeds are toasted and the center is rare, 4 to 7 minutes, flipping halfway through. (If the tuna is much thinner, about ½ inch thick, it will take about 2 minutes.)

Meanwhile, in a small bowl, whisk together the mayo and wasabi paste. If needed, thin out the mixture with water until it's the consistency you like.

As soon as the tuna comes out of the air fryer, squeeze a bit of lemon juice over it. Serve immediately over arugula with the wasabi mayo on the side.

PER SERVING: **1 tuna steak + 1 cup arugula + about 1 tablespoon wasabi mayo** • CALORIES **306** • FAT **12 g** • SATURATED FAT **2 g** • CHOLESTEROL **79 mg** • CARBOHYDRATE **6 g** • FIBER **2 g** • PROTEIN **42 g** • SUGARS **1 g** • SODIUM **326 mg**

BACON-WRAPPED SCALLOPS

SERVES 4

8 slices center-cut bacon, halved crosswise

16 large sea scallops (about 1 pound)

Olive oil spray

Freshly ground black pepper

Scallops are so meaty and delicious, and they take just minutes to cook, which makes this a perfect weeknight dish. In the air fryer, the scallops come out juicy and tender on the inside, with the bacon crispy and golden on the outside—all in under 10 minutes. To get perfectly crisp bacon without overcooking the scallops, I partially cook the bacon in the air fryer for a few minutes before wrapping the scallops. I love serving this with a salad and Mushrooms with Frizzled Shallots and Bacon (page 155), Roasted Balsamic Asparagus (page 152), or Golden Breaded Cauliflower (page 144).

Preheat the air fryer to 400°F for 3 minutes.

Add the bacon to the air fryer basket in a single layer. Cook until the bacon is partially crisped but still pliable, about 3 minutes, flipping halfway through. Transfer the bacon to a paper towel to cool.

Remove any side muscles on the scallops. Pat the scallops dry with paper towels to remove any excess moisture.

Wrap each scallop in a half slice of bacon and secure it with a toothpick. Spritz the scallops all over with oil and season lightly with black pepper.

Working in batches, arrange the scallops in the air fryer basket in a single layer. Cook until the scallops are tender and opaque and the bacon is cooked through, about 8 minutes, flipping halfway through. Serve hot.

PER SERVING: 4 wrapped scallops · CALORIES 138 · FAT 5 g · SATURATED FAT 1.5 g · CHOLESTEROL 32 mg · CARBOHYDRATE 4 g · FIBER 0 g · PROTEIN 19 g · SUGARS 0 g · SODIUM 685 mg

SHRIMP TEMPURA SUSHI "BURRITOS"

SERVES 4

2 cups cooked brown rice, warmed

1 tablespoon unseasoned rice vinegar

1½ teaspoons sugar

Kosher salt

¾ cup (4 ounces) snow crab meat or flake-style surimi (imitation crab)

4 ounces avocado (about 1 small)

Juice of ½ lime

1 large egg

¾ cup plain panko bread crumbs, wheat or gluten-free

8 peeled extra-jumbo tiger shrimp (about ¾ pound)

Olive oil spray

4 toasted nori sheets (look for premium quality)

2 teaspoons toasted sesame seeds

1 jalapeño pepper, seeded and sliced into thin strips

½ English cucumber, cut into 2- to 3-inch matchsticks (about ⅔ cup)

Reduced-sodium soy sauce or gluten-free tamari, for serving (optional)

The surprising flavor combo of this burrito-size sushi roll is so delicious—jalapeños, avocado, and lime pair perfectly with the nori, cucumbers, and snow crab. For a light dinner, serve this with a salad or some steamed edamame. You can also slice the burrito into 8 pieces and eat it, sushi-style, with chopsticks.

Place the rice in a medium bowl and stir in the vinegar, sugar, and ½ teaspoon of the salt. Set aside while you assemble the other ingredients.

If you're using snow crab, flake it with your fingers. If you're using surimi, finely chop it. In a small bowl, mash the avocado with the lime juice and ¼ teaspoon of the salt.

In a shallow bowl, lightly beat the egg. In a separate bowl, combine the panko with ½ teaspoon salt.

Pat the shrimp dry with paper towels. Dip them into the egg mixture, letting any excess drop back into the bowl, then toss to coat in the panko, pressing to help adhere. Spritz both sides of the shrimp with oil.

Working in batches if needed, arrange the shrimp in the air fryer basket in a single layer. Cook at 400°F until the panko crust is golden, 6 to 8 minutes, flipping halfway through. Cut each breaded shrimp in half.

To assemble the burritos, set a piece of plastic wrap (or parchment paper) on a work surface and fill a small dish or bowl with water to keep nearby. Arrange 1 nori sheet, shiny side down, on top of the plastic.

Scoop ½ cup rice onto the sheet and use wet fingers to spread it out in as even a layer as you can, leaving about a 1-inch border from the bottom edge and the sides. Sprinkle ½ teaspoon sesame seeds over the rice.

Dividing evenly, arrange the avocado mixture, jalapeño, and cucumber in a row along the bottom edge of the rice and top with the crab. Arrange 4 tempura shrimp halves end to end on top of the crab.

PER SERVING: 1 "burrito" • CALORIES 277 • FAT 7 g • SATURATED FAT 1 g • CHOLESTEROL 176 mg • CARBOHYDRATE 35 g • FIBER 5 g • PROTEIN 24 g • SUGARS 5 g • SODIUM 584 mg

Lift the plastic under the burrito and use it to coax the nori around the filling, then continue to roll it up like a burrito, using the plastic wrap to snuggle the nori tightly around the filling. Wet the edge with water and press to seal. Set aside and repeat with the remaining nori and fillings. Serve with the soy sauce for dipping, if desired.

FRIED CATFISH AND HUSHPUPPIES WITH CREAMY SLAW

SERVES 4

Classic Southern fried catfish and hushpuppies get a healthy makeover in the air fryer! Soaking the catfish in buttermilk not only sweetens the fish, but it's also the perfect coating for the cornmeal crust. The hushpuppies have a slightly different texture than the traditionally deep-fried version, but they're less greasy and just as delicious.

1 cup light buttermilk

½ teaspoon hot sauce

4 catfish fillets (6 ounces each)

HUSHPUPPIES

½ cup cornmeal

½ cup all-purpose flour

¾ teaspoon kosher salt

1½ teaspoons baking powder

⅛ teaspoon cayenne pepper

⅓ cup finely diced onion

⅓ cup finely diced
red bell pepper

½ cup plus 2 teaspoons
whole milk

Olive oil spray

FRIED FISH

Olive oil spray

¾ cup cornmeal

¼ cup plus 2 tablespoons
all-purpose flour

2 tablespoons Old Bay

¾ teaspoon garlic powder

¾ teaspoon onion powder

1¼ teaspoons kosher salt

SLAW

4 cups coleslaw mix

¼ cup light buttermilk

1 tablespoon diced onion

1½ tablespoons apple
cider vinegar

½ tablespoon olive oil

½ teaspoon kosher salt

FOR SERVING

4 lemon wedges

1 teaspoon honey (optional)

In a large shallow dish, combine the buttermilk and hot sauce. Add the catfish fillets, cover the dish with plastic wrap, and refrigerate for at least 1 hour or up to 8 hours, flipping once.

Preheat the oven to 250°F.

FOR THE HUSHPUPPIES: In a medium bowl, combine the cornmeal, flour, salt, baking powder, and cayenne. Stir in the onion, bell pepper, and milk until a uniform dough forms. Cover and chill the dough in the freezer for 15 minutes.

Remove the air fryer basket and cover it with air fryer parchment paper (see page 11). Lightly spritz the parchment with oil.

Working in batches, scoop the hushpuppies dough in heaping tablespoonfuls and place about 1 inch apart on the parchment. Lightly spritz them with oil. Cook until the hushpuppies are golden, 10 to 12 minutes, flipping halfway through. Transfer the hushpuppies to the oven to keep warm.

FOR FRYING THE FISH: Discard the parchment and lightly spritz the air fryer basket with olive oil. In a shallow dish, combine the cornmeal, flour, Old Bay, garlic powder, onion powder, and salt. Remove the fish fillets from the buttermilk mixture and shake off any excess. Dredge the fillets in the cornmeal mixture and shake off any excess. Working in batches, add the fillets to the air fryer basket in a single layer and spritz with oil. Cook at 400°F for 7 minutes. Flip and continue cooking until the crust is golden and the fish is opaque, about 3 minutes more.

MEANWHILE, FOR THE SLAW: In a large bowl, combine the slaw mix, buttermilk, diced onion, vinegar, olive oil, and salt.

TO SERVE: Transfer the fish to a platter and serve with the slaw, lemon wedges, and hushpuppies. Drizzle the hushpuppies with honey, if desired.

PER SERVING: 1 piece of catfish + 4 hushpuppies + 1 cup slaw · CALORIES 395 · FAT 9 g · SATURATED FAT 2.5 g · CHOLESTEROL 103 mg · CARBOHYDRATE 44 g · FIBER 4.5 g · PROTEIN 35 g · SUGARS 6 g · SODIUM 1,121 mg

CAJUN SHRIMP DINNER

SERVES 4

1 pound peeled and deveined extra-jumbo wild shrimp (about 24 shrimp)

1 tablespoon Cajun or Creole seasoning*

6 ounces fully cooked turkey or chicken andouille sausage or kielbasa,* sliced

1 medium zucchini (8 ounces), sliced into ¼-inch-thick half-moons

1 medium yellow squash (8 ounces), sliced into ¼-inch-thick half-moons

1 large red bell pepper, cut into 1-inch pieces

¼ teaspoon kosher salt

2 tablespoons extra-virgin olive oil

*Read the label to be sure this product is gluten-free.

This easy one-and-done dish is my favorite type of meal for weeknight cooking. Made with shrimp, sausage, and lots of colorful vegetables tossed with tasty Cajun spices, it's packed with flavor. The best part is that it takes less than 30 minutes to get dinner on the table. Serve this over rice to round out the meal.

In a large bowl, combine the shrimp and Cajun seasoning and toss to coat. Add the sausage, zucchini, yellow squash, bell pepper, salt, and olive oil. Toss again to coat.

Preheat the air fryer to 400°F.

Working in two batches if needed, add the shrimp and sausage mixture to the air fryer basket in a single layer and cook, shaking the basket 2 to 3 times, until the shrimp are pink and cooked through and the vegetables are tender-crisp, about 8 minutes. Transfer the first batch to a plate and repeat with the remaining mixture. Once both batches are cooked, return the first batch to the air fryer and cook for 1 minute more just to warm through.

Divide among four plates or bowls and serve immediately.

PER SERVING: 1½ cups · CALORIES 292 · FAT 15 g · SATURATED FAT 4 g · CHOLESTEROL 193 mg · CARBOHYDRATE 7 g · FIBER 2 g · PROTEIN 32 g · SUGARS 5 g · SODIUM 793 mg

BLACKENED FISH TACOS

SERVES 4

CHIPOTLE MAYONNAISE

⅓ cup light mayonnaise

1 tablespoon minced canned chipotle pepper in adobo sauce

PICO DE GALLO

1½ cups chopped tomatoes

⅔ cup chopped onion

⅓ cup chopped fresh cilantro

Juice of 1 lime

¼ teaspoon kosher salt

TACOS

1 tablespoon sweet paprika

1 teaspoon garlic powder

1 teaspoon dried oregano

1 teaspoon dried thyme

1 teaspoon kosher salt

½ teaspoon cayenne pepper

⅛ teaspoon freshly ground black pepper

4 pieces white-fleshed fish fillet (about 6 ounces each), such as mahimahi, grouper, or red snapper

Olive oil spray

12 (6-inch) corn tortillas

3 cups chopped green cabbage or coleslaw mix

Meet my new favorite fish taco! These are inspired by the Florida Keys, where I eat "catch of the day" fish tacos every chance I get when we visit. Simply prepared with blackened mahimahi, pico de gallo, cabbage, and a drizzle of chipotle sauce, these tacos pack a ton of flavor into every bite. In New York, I can get only frozen mahimahi, which works great for this recipe, but I always suggest you use whatever fish is freshest or in season where you live.

FOR THE CHIPOTLE MAYONNAISE: In a small bowl, whisk the mayonnaise, chipotle, and 2 tablespoons water until smooth.

FOR THE PICO DE GALLO: In a medium bowl, combine all of the ingredients and toss gently.

FOR THE TACOS: In a small bowl, stir together the paprika, garlic powder, oregano, thyme, salt, cayenne, and pepper.

Cut each piece of fish into 3 strips and place on a large plate or parchment. Spritz the fish with oil on both sides and rub all over. Coat both sides with the spice mixture.

Spritz the air fryer basket with oil. Working in batches, arrange the fish in the air fryer basket in a single layer. Cook at 400°F until the fish flakes easily with a fork, 5 to 7 minutes (depending on the thickness of the fish), flipping halfway through.

Meanwhile, heat the tortillas and keep warm (I like to char over an open flame on my gas stove, a few seconds per side).

Just before serving, drain the pico de gallo in a fine-mesh sieve (so the tortillas don't get soggy). Divide the tortillas among four plates. Top each with 1 piece of fish and some of the chopped cabbage and drained pico de gallo. Drizzle each taco with about 2 teaspoons of the chipotle mayonnaise and serve.

PER SERVING: **3 tacos with toppings** · CALORIES **535** · FAT **23 g** · SATURATED FAT **7 g** · CHOLESTEROL **88 mg** · CARBOHYDRATE **46 g** · FIBER **8.5 g** · PROTEIN **38 g** · SUGARS **7 g** · SODIUM **705 mg**

FRIED SHRIMP PO'BOY WRAPS

SERVES 4

1½ cups shredded red or green cabbage

1 tablespoon Creole mustard

1 tablespoon fresh lemon juice

¼ teaspoon kosher salt

¼ cup light mayonnaise

2 teaspoons Tabasco or other Louisiana-style hot sauce

16 peeled colossal wild shrimp (about ¾ pound; see Skinny Scoop)

1½ teaspoons Creole seasoning

½ cup all-purpose flour

2 large eggs

1 cup panko bread crumbs

Olive oil spray

4 large (10-inch) low-carb flour tortillas

1 small tomato, thinly sliced

1 cup dill pickle slices (see Skinny Scoop)

Skinny Scoop: I love the tangy bite from the pickles, but if you are watching your sodium intake, you can cut back on them.

In New Orleans, traditional po'boy sandwiches are served on big, hearty rolls. This po'boy wrap cuts back on the carbs, but keeps all the signature flavors and textures. A little heat from the Tabasco, tanginess from the pickles, and great crunch from the dressed cabbage—all accompany the big, juicy shrimp.

In a medium bowl, combine the cabbage, Creole mustard, lemon juice, and salt. Use your hands to mix thoroughly and work the dressing into the cabbage.

In a small bowl, whisk the mayonnaise and hot sauce until smooth.

Pat the shrimp dry with paper towels. Season both sides with the Creole seasoning. Place the flour in a shallow bowl or on a plate. In a separate shallow bowl, beat the eggs. Place the panko in a third shallow bowl.

Working in batches, dredge the shrimp in the flour, shaking off any excess. Dip the shrimp in the egg until coated, letting the excess drip back into the bowl. Dredge the shrimp in the panko and press to adhere.

Spritz the air fryer basket with oil. Arrange the shrimp in the air fryer basket in a single layer and spritz the tops with oil. Cook at 400°F for 3 minutes. Flip, spray the tops of the shrimp again, and continue cooking until the panko crust is golden, about 2 to 3 minutes more.

Heat a large skillet over medium heat. Working with one tortilla at a time, toast until just warm and pliable, 10 to 15 seconds per side.

To assemble the wraps, divide the tortillas among plates. Spread about 1 tablespoon spicy mayonnaise in the center of each tortilla, leaving a couple of inches on the bottom edge for rolling. Add the cabbage mixture, 2 to 3 slices of tomato, and a few dill pickle slices on top. Top each with 4 shrimp. Fold the bottom edge of the tortilla over the filling, then tightly roll in the sides. Serve immediately.

PER SERVING: 1 wrap · CALORIES 341 · FAT 10 g · SATURATED FAT 2 g · CHOLESTEROL 221 mg · CARBOHYDRATE 39 g · FIBER 14.5 g · PROTEIN 31 g · SUGARS 4 g · SODIUM 1,185 mg

GNOCCHI
WITH SHRIMP AND BURST TOMATOES

SERVES 4

1 (16-ounce) package shelf-stable gnocchi, regular or gluten-free

1 pound peeled and deveined large shrimp

1 teaspoon kosher salt

5 large garlic cloves, slightly smashed

¼ teaspoon crushed red pepper flakes, plus more for topping

2 pints cherry or grape tomatoes, halved

2 tablespoons extra-virgin olive oil

Olive oil spray

Chopped fresh basil, for garnish

Pecorino Romano, for serving (optional)

Gnocchi are an Italian pasta typically made with cooked mashed potatoes, flour, and eggs. Air-frying store-bought gnocchi is so easy—it doesn't require any boiling! Just wet the gnocchi and cook in the air fryer, and they'll magically transform into perfectly cooked dumplings that are crispy on the outside and chewy on the inside. This one-pot dish is studded with garlic, tomatoes, and shrimp that cook together into a jammy, tasty sauce. Finish it with basil and a good grating cheese like Pecorino Romano.

Place the gnocchi in a large bowl, cover with water to submerge, and let sit for 1 minute. Drain in a colander and return to the bowl. Add the shrimp, salt, garlic, pepper flakes, tomatoes, and oil and toss to combine.

Spritz the air fryer basket with oil. Working in batches, add half of the gnocchi/shrimp mixture to the air fryer basket and spritz a few times with oil. Cook at 400°F until the shrimp are opaque, the gnocchi are tender, and the tomatoes burst, about 8 minutes, shaking the basket halfway through. Transfer to a serving bowl and repeat with the second batch.

Stir everything together until saucy. Top with the basil and Pecorino, if desired, and serve.

PER SERVING: 1½ generous cups · CALORIES 365 · FAT 16 g · SATURATED FAT 6.5 g · CHOLESTEROL 186 mg · CARBOHYDRATE 27 g · FIBER 3 g · PROTEIN 27 g · SUGARS 5 g · SODIUM 741 mg

SWEET AND SPICY GLAZED SALMON

SERVES 4

4 wild salmon fillets
(about 4 ounces each)

¼ teaspoon kosher salt

¼ cup Thai sweet chili sauce

1 teaspoon Sriracha
sauce, or more to taste

½ teaspoon grated
fresh ginger

Olive oil spray

¼ cup sliced scallions,
for garnish

I love salmon, but it's pretty hard for me to choose a favorite recipe because I have so many! This one comes close, though—when I tested this recipe, I instantly fell in love. The easy homemade salmon glaze packs so much flavor with just three ingredients. The chili sauce adds sweetness and caramelization, the Sriracha adds a little heat, and the ginger gives it a warm flavor. Serve this with brown rice and steamed baby bok choy or broccoli.

Season the salmon with the salt. In a small bowl, combine the chili sauce, Sriracha, and ginger and mix to combine. Brush on top of the salmon.

Spritz the air fryer basket generously with oil. Working in batches as needed, place the salmon in the air fryer basket in a single layer. Cook at 400°F until the salmon is cooked through, 7 to 8 minutes.

To serve, transfer the salmon to a serving plate and garnish with the scallions.

PER SERVING: **1 piece** · CALORIES **200** · FAT **7 g** · SATURATED FAT **1 g** · CHOLESTEROL **62 mg** · CARBOHYDRATE **10 g** · FIBER **0 g** · PROTEIN **23 g** · SUGARS **7 g** · SODIUM **360 mg**

FRIED FISH FILLET SANDWICHES

SERVES 4

Q

I re-created the popular fast-food fish fillet sandwich, which also happens to be one of Tommy's favorites! The fish came out so perfectly—crisp on the outside, yet tender and flaky on the inside. A soft potato bun slathered with a homemade dill tartar sauce and filled with crisp lettuce holds it all together. Is your mouth watering yet? I even included the half strip of cheese to mimic the Golden Arches' version.

DILL TARTAR SAUCE

1/4 cup reduced-fat sour cream

3 tablespoons light mayonnaise

1/3 cup finely chopped dill pickle

1 tablespoon fresh chopped dill

1 teaspoon fresh lemon juice

1/8 teaspoon kosher salt

FISH

1 pound skinless haddock fillets (see Skinny Scoop)

1 teaspoon kosher salt

2 large egg whites, lightly beaten

1 cup panko bread crumbs

Olive oil spray

2 slices American or cheddar cheese, cut in half

4 whole wheat potato buns

1/2 cup chopped iceberg or romaine lettuce

FOR THE DILL TARTAR SAUCE: In a small bowl, combine all the ingredients and refrigerate until ready to eat.

FOR THE FISH: Pat the fish dry with paper towels. Cut the fish into 4 pieces total (a size that will fit nicely on the potato bun). Season with 1/2 teaspoon of the salt.

Place the egg whites in a shallow bowl. In a second shallow bowl, combine the panko with the remaining 1/2 teaspoon salt. Dip the fish into the egg whites, then the panko. Set aside.

Spritz the air fryer basket with oil. Working in batches as needed, place the fish in the air fryer basket in a single layer. Spritz the tops of the fish with oil. Cook at 400°F for 4 minutes. Flip, spritz the tops with oil again, and continue cooking until golden and crisp, about 4 minutes more. Top the fish with the cheese slices and cook for about 1 minute until melted.

Spread 2 1/2 tablespoons tartar sauce on the bottom of each bun. Serve the fish on the buns topped with the lettuce.

Skinny Scoop: If you can't find haddock, any white-fleshed fish fillet, such as cod or halibut, will work.

PER SERVING: **1 sandwich** · CALORIES **345** · FAT **12 g** · SATURATED FAT **5 g** · CHOLESTEROL **83 mg** · CARBOHYDRATE **27 g** · FIBER **2.5 g** · PROTEIN **32 g** · SUGARS **6 g** · SODIUM **977 mg**

LOBSTER TAILS
WITH GARLIC-PARPRIKA BUTTER

SERVES 4

4 lobster tails (4 ounces each), thawed if frozen

2 tablespoons salted butter or nondairy butter

1 large garlic clove, grated

¼ teaspoon sweet paprika

Chopped fresh parsley, for garnish (optional)

1 lemon, cut into wedges, for serving

Lobster tails are so much easier to cook than you think, I promise! Nothing is worse than spending money on lobster tails, only to be disappointed when they come out dry or rubbery. Well, good news: Once you make them in the air fryer, you'll never fear wasting money on lobster again. You get perfectly cooked lobster every single time. Serve these tails with corn on the cob, Lemon Potatoes (page 168), or a salad or slaw on the side to make it a meal.

Using kitchen shears, cut the top shell and flesh of the lobster lengthwise, right through the meat, leaving the bottom of the shell uncut. Spread the halves of the tails apart and place in the air fryer basket, cut side up. Cook at 380°F until the lobster is opaque, 5 to 7 minutes. If the tails are bigger, add 1 to 2 minutes.

Meanwhile, in a small skillet, melt the butter over medium-low heat. Add the garlic and cook on low heat until fragrant but not browned, 1 to 2 minutes. Add the paprika and remove from the heat.

Brush the butter over the lobster meat just before serving. Garnish with the parsley, if desired, and serve with the lemon wedges.

PER SERVING: **1 lobster tail** · CALORIES **144** · FAT **7 g** · SATURATED FAT **4 g** · CHOLESTEROL **159 mg** · CARBOHYDRATE **2 g** · FIBER **0.5 g** · PROTEIN **19 g** · SUGARS **0.5 g** · SODIUM **526 mg**

TZATZIKI FISH TACOS

SERVES 4

Q GF

Since my family is obsessed with tzatziki sauce (we eat it with everything!), I thought why not make fish tacos with a Greek twist? I breaded the fish strips for extra crunch, and served the crispy fish on tortillas with shredded cabbage, chopped tomatoes, and diced red onions, all topped with homemade tzatziki—so delicious (and no judgment if you use store-bought sauce to save time!).

MINT TZATZIKI SAUCE

1 medium cucumber, peeled and seeded

¾ cup 0% Greek yogurt

1 small clove garlic, grated

1 teaspoon fresh lemon juice

½ tablespoon chopped fresh mint

½ tablespoon chopped fresh dill

¼ teaspoon plus ⅛ teaspoon kosher salt

Freshly ground black pepper

FISH

12 ounces skinless white-fleshed fish fillets, such as cod, mahimahi, or haddock

1 teaspoon kosher salt

1 tablespoon flour, all-purpose or gluten-free

1 large egg, beaten

½ cup plain panko bread crumbs, wheat or gluten-free

¼ teaspoon garlic powder

¼ teaspoon dried oregano

Olive oil spray

TACOS

2 cups chopped green cabbage

8 small (street taco size) tortillas, flour or corn, warmed (I like Mission)

1 tomato, diced

¼ cup diced red onion

Chopped fresh dill, for topping

8 lemon wedges, for serving

FOR THE MINT TZATZIKI SAUCE: Pulse the cucumber in a mini food processor or coarsely grate on a box grater. Drain the cucumber in a fine-mesh sieve, using the back of a spoon to help press out any excess liquid (you'll have about ⅓ cup cucumber).

In a medium bowl, combine the grated cucumber with the yogurt, garlic, lemon juice, mint, dill, salt, and pepper to taste. Refrigerate until ready to eat.

FOR THE FISH: Cut the fish into 8 strips total and season with ½ teaspoon of the salt.

Place the flour on a plate and the egg in a shallow bowl. On another plate, combine the panko with the remaining ½ teaspoon salt, the garlic powder, and oregano.

Preheat the air fryer to 400°F.

Coat the fish pieces in the flour, shaking off any excess. Dip the fish into the egg, then into the panko. Transfer to a board lined with parchment or wax paper. Spritz both sides of the fish with oil.

Working in batches, place the fish in the air fryer basket in a single layer. Cook at 400°F until golden and crisp, 6 to 8 minutes, flipping halfway through.

FOR THE TACOS: Place ¼ cup cabbage on each tortilla. Top with a piece of fish, some tzatziki, tomato, red onion, a sprinkle of dill, and a squeeze of fresh lemon juice and serve.

PER SERVING: **2 tacos** • CALORIES **306** • FAT **5 g** • SATURATED FAT **1.5 g** • CHOLESTEROL **89 mg** • CARBOHYDRATE **40 g** • FIBER **3 g** • PROTEIN **25 g** • SUGARS **6 g** • SODIUM **1,130 mg**

SIDES

GOLDEN BREADED CAULIFLOWER

SERVES 4

⅓ cup all-purpose flour

1 teaspoon garlic salt

2 large eggs

½ cup panko bread crumbs

½ cup finely grated Parmesan cheese

Olive oil spray

1 small head cauliflower, stemmed and cut into small (1½-inch) florets (about 32 pieces)

Lemon wedges, for serving

Growing up, I loved it whenever my mom made us deep-fried cauliflower! Putting the air fryer to the test, I couldn't believe how amazing this version tasted, even with just a little oil. For the breading, I did equal parts panko and finely grated Parmesan. A squeeze of lemon is a must at the end. This dish is also such a perfect way to get the kiddos to eat more veggies!

Place the flour in a shallow dish and whisk in ½ teaspoon of the garlic salt. In a second shallow dish, beat the eggs with 1 tablespoon water and season with the remaining ½ teaspoon garlic salt. In a third shallow dish, combine the panko and Parmesan.

Spritz the air fryer basket with oil. Working with a few florets at a time, dredge the cauliflower in the flour, shaking off the excess. Dip in the egg mixture, then roll in the panko/Parmesan mixture. Transfer half of the cauliflower to the air fryer basket and spritz the tops generously with oil. Cook at 360°F for 5 minutes. Flip, spritz them again with oil, and continue cooking until the cauliflower is golden and tender, about 5 minutes more.

Transfer the cauliflower to a serving plate and serve immediately, with lemon wedges alongside.

PER SERVING: **8 florets** · CALORIES **146** · FAT **6 g** · SATURATED FAT **2.5 g** · CHOLESTEROL **104 mg** · CARBOHYDRATE **14 g** · FIBER **2 g** · PROTEIN **9 g** · SUGARS **2 g** · SODIUM **532 mg**

SMASHED POTATOES

SERVES 4

12 baby gold potatoes
(about 1 pound)

1 teaspoon extra-
virgin olive oil

½ teaspoon kosher salt

½ teaspoon freshly
ground black pepper

Chopped fresh
parsley, for garnish

These smashed potatoes are tender on the inside and crisp on the outside—the perfect side dish to any meal. Try them with Swedish Turkey Meatballs (page 70) or Gouda-Stuffed Beef and Mushroom Burgers (page 103). Since the potatoes are partially cooked in the microwave, this cuts down the air-fry time. So, you can air-fry your protein while the potatoes cook in the microwave, then while the protein rests, crisp up the potatoes in the air fryer.

Place the potatoes in a microwave-safe dish and cover with cold water. Microwave until a knife easily pierces to the center of each potato, 8 to 9 minutes. Drain the potatoes and pat dry. Place the potatoes on a clean work surface and gently press using the bottom of a glass to smash the potato to about a 1-inch thickness.

Lightly brush the potatoes all over with the oil and sprinkle both sides of each potato with the salt and pepper (see Skinny Scoop).

Working in batches if needed, place the potatoes in the air fryer basket in a single layer. Cook at 400°F until crisp and golden, 10 to 12 minutes, flipping halfway through. Transfer the potatoes to a serving dish and garnish with the parsley.

Skinny Scoop: You can also season the potatoes with fresh thyme, rosemary, Parmesan, or lemon zest.

PER SERVING: **3 potatoes** • CALORIES **89** • FAT **1 g** • SATURATED FAT **0 g** • CHOLESTEROL **0 mg** •
CARBOHYDRATE **18 g** • FIBER **3 g** • PROTEIN **2 g** • SUGARS **1 g** • SODIUM **159 mg**

BLISTERED ASIAN-STYLE GREEN BEANS

SERVES 4

1 pound green beans, rinsed, trimmed, and patted dry

1 tablespoon vegetable or canola oil

¼ cup reduced-sodium soy sauce or gluten-free tamari

1 tablespoon grated fresh ginger

2 garlic cloves, minced

1 tablespoon hoisin*

2 teaspoons sambal oelek (chile paste)

½ teaspoon toasted sesame oil

2 tablespoons unseasoned rice vinegar

*Read the label to be sure this product is gluten-free.

This side dish is inspired by the Sichuan green beans I love at some of my favorite Chinese restaurants. I found out that the secret is the beans are often deep-fried before tossed in their delicious, salty, spicy sauce. No deep-frying needed in this version! The air fryer is the perfect answer—it blisters the beans before they're coated in the sauce, making an all-in-one air fryer basket dish.

Preheat the air fryer to 400°F.

In a large bowl, combine the green beans and vegetable oil. Toss to evenly coat.

Working in batches, add the green beans to the air fryer basket in a single layer. (Do not overcrowd the basket or the beans won't blister.) Cook until the beans are starting to blacken and blister, 4 to 5 minutes. Transfer the finished beans to a large bowl and repeat with the remaining beans.

Meanwhile, in a small bowl, combine the soy sauce, ginger, garlic, hoisin, sambal oelek, sesame oil, and vinegar and whisk together.

Pour the sauce over the beans and toss to evenly coat. Return the beans, along with the sauce, to the air fryer in one big batch. Cook for 2 minutes at 400°F to heat the beans through and meld the flavors.

Transfer the beans to a serving platter, along with any sauce in the bottom of the basket. Toss one more time to combine and serve immediately.

PER SERVING: ⅔ cup · CALORIES 94 · FAT 4 g · SATURATED FAT 0.5 g · CHOLESTEROL 0 mg · CARBOHYDRATE 12 g · FIBER 4 g · PROTEIN 3 g · SUGARS 3 g · SODIUM 662 mg

CHEESY BROCCOLI POTATO PATTIES

SERVES 6

1 (8-ounce) russet potato, rinsed

½ tablespoon extra-virgin olive oil

3 medium or 2 large leeks, white parts only, washed and sliced into ½-inch-thick rounds

1 large garlic clove, smashed with the side of a knife

4 ounces cooked broccoli florets (thawed frozen or steamed fresh)

6 tablespoons (1½ ounces) shredded cheddar cheese or nondairy cheddar (such as Violife)

1 large egg

¾ teaspoon kosher salt

Olive oil spray

Here's a great way to get kids (and adults of all ages!) to eat their veggies. These easy potato patties are mixed with leeks, broccoli, and cheese. I've also tested them with dairy-free cheddar cheese, and they taste just as delicious. Leftover patties can be frozen up to 3 months.

Pierce the potato all over with a fork. Microwave until tender and cooked through, 4 to 5 minutes. Let the potato cool before peeling and slicing in half.

Meanwhile, in a medium bowl, combine the oil, leeks (don't separate the rings), and garlic and toss to coat. Place the leek mixture in the air fryer basket and cook at 370°F until the leeks are soft, about 6 minutes.

While the leeks are cooking, transfer half of the potato to a large bowl and mash with a fork. Cut the other half of the potato into ⅛-inch dice (or, if you have one, use an egg slicer and slice in both directions). Add the diced potato to the bowl with the mashed potato.

Transfer the leek/garlic mixture to a food processor. Add the broccoli and pulse until finely chopped. Add to the bowl with the potatoes, along with the cheddar, egg, and salt and mix until just combined.

Form the mixture into 6 balls, each about ⅓ cup (3 ounces). Flatten them into patties about ½ inch thick. Spritz both sides of each patty with oil.

Working in batches if needed, place the patties in the air fryer basket in a single layer. Cook at 400°F until golden, 6 to 8 minutes, flipping halfway through. Serve immediately.

PER SERVING: **1 patty** • CALORIES **101** • FAT **4 g** • SATURATED FAT **2 g** • CHOLESTEROL **38 mg** • CARBOHYDRATE **12 g** • FIBER **2 g** • PROTEIN **4 g** • SUGARS **2 g** • SODIUM **216 mg**

ROASTED BALSAMIC ASPARAGUS

SERVES 4

20 asparagus spears
(about 1 bunch), tough ends
trimmed (see Skinny Scoop)

2 teaspoons extra-
virgin olive oil

1 tablespoon balsamic vinegar

¼ teaspoon plus
⅛ teaspoon kosher salt

1 garlic clove, minced
or grated

2 teaspoons dried parsley

I love roasting vegetables in the air fryer—they get charred and crisp on the edges, transforming just about any veggie into healthy deliciousness in minutes. Marinating vegetables in Italian dressing is also one of my favorite ways to add flavor. Here, a simple balsamic marinade pairs nicely with asparagus, but you can also use it with zucchini, bell peppers, or whatever veggies you happen to have on hand.

In a large bowl, toss the asparagus with the olive oil, balsamic, ¼ teaspoon of the salt, the garlic, and parsley until well coated. Set aside to marinate for 10 to 15 minutes.

Working in batches if needed, add the asparagus to the air fryer basket in a single layer. Cook at 400°F until slightly charred on the edges, 8 to 10 minutes (depending on the thickness), shaking the basket halfway through.

Transfer the asparagus to a serving dish and sprinkle with the remaining ⅛ teaspoon salt before serving.

Skinny Scoop: To keep asparagus fresh and hydrated until I'm ready to cook, I trim the ends off and keep them upright in a jar of water in the refrigerator, just like freshly cut flowers.

PER SERVING: **5 spears** · CALORIES **41** · FAT **2 g** · SATURATED FAT **0.5 g** · CHOLESTEROL **0 mg** · CARBOHYDRATE **4 g** · FIBER **2 g** · PROTEIN **2 g** · SUGARS **2 g** · SODIUM **109 mg**

MUSHROOMS
WITH FRIZZLED SHALLOTS AND BACON

SERVES 4

1 pound white mushrooms, sliced

1 large shallot, halved and cut into ¼-inch-thick slices

2 tablespoons extra-virgin olive oil

½ teaspoon kosher salt

Freshly ground black pepper

3 slices center-cut bacon, chopped into ¼-inch pieces

Juice of 1 lemon

Fresh herbs, such as chives, parsley, or thyme, for garnish

These mushrooms taste divine and are so incredibly easy to make! I combine them with garlic, shallots, and bacon and then toss them in the air fryer (no messy skillet!) for the most delicious side dish. The shallots get caramelized and crisp—aka "frizzled." Pair this side with just about anything; try it with Prosciutto-Wrapped Pork Tenderloin (page 92) or Juicy Brined Pork Chops (page 104), or toss them with whole grains or pasta. You can also serve the mushrooms as an appetizer on a toasted baguette or eat them straight up. The possibilities are endless!

In a large bowl, combine the mushrooms, shallot, oil, salt, and pepper to taste. Add the bacon and toss to combine.

Place the mushroom mixture in the air fryer basket. Cook at 380°F, stirring every 5 minutes, until the mushrooms are caramelized and the shallots and bacon are crisp, about 22 minutes. (If using a smaller air fryer basket, cook the mushrooms in two batches, shaking halfway, 12 minutes total.)

Transfer to a serving platter or bowl. Top with the lemon juice and garnish with the fresh herbs before serving.

PER SERVING: ½ cup • CALORIES **124** • FAT **9 g** • SATURATED FAT **1.5 g** • CHOLESTEROL **2 mg** • CARBOHYDRATE **8 g** • FIBER **2 g** • PROTEIN **6 g** • SUGARS **4 g** • SODIUM **238 mg**

EGGPLANT FRIES

SERVES 4

12 ounces eggplant
(about 1 medium)

1 teaspoon extra-
virgin olive oil

½ teaspoon kosher salt

Freshly ground black pepper

½ cup plus 2 tablespoons
Italian seasoned bread
crumbs, wheat or gluten-free

2 tablespoons freshly
grated Parmesan cheese

2 large eggs

Olive oil spray

Marinara sauce (store-bought
or homemade), warmed,
for dipping (optional)

I can vividly remember the day when Karina, my oldest daughter who was such a picky eater as a kid, told me she liked eggplant. Eggplant? Really?! She was eating dinner at a friend's house, and they served fried breaded eggplant for dinner. She loved it. Kids are always more willing to try new foods when they are eating away from home, right? I was so excited about this new vegetable she was eating that I made her these breaded eggplant fries at least once a month! This is one of the easiest, tastiest ways to eat eggplant as a side dish, snack, or appetizer.

Cut the eggplant into 24 sticks, 4 to 5 inches long and ½ inch thick. Place the sticks in a large bowl and toss with the olive oil, salt, and pepper to taste.

In a shallow bowl, combine the bread crumbs and Parmesan. In another shallow bowl, beat the eggs.

Spritz the air fryer basket with oil. Working with a few pieces of eggplant at a time, dip the eggplant into the egg, then into the bread crumb mixture.

Use a fork to remove the eggplant from the bread crumb mixture and place the eggplant in the air fryer basket in a single layer. Spritz the strips with oil. Cook at 350°F until the eggplant is golden and crisp, about 10 minutes, flipping halfway through.

Serve the eggplant with marinara sauce for dipping, if desired.

PER SERVING: **6 pieces** · CALORIES **127** · FAT **5 g** · SATURATED FAT **1.5 g** · CHOLESTEROL **95 mg** ·
CARBOHYDRATE **14 g** · FIBER **4 g** · PROTEIN **7 g** · SUGARS **3 g** · SODIUM **512 mg**

GARLIC CHEDDAR BISCUITS

SERVES 4

1 cup all-purpose flour, plus more for dusting

1½ teaspoons baking powder

¾ teaspoon kosher salt

2 tablespoons salted whipped butter

½ cup 0% Greek yogurt

1 ounce reduced-fat shredded cheddar cheese

2 garlic cloves, minced or grated

Olive oil spray

1 tablespoon finely chopped fresh parsley

Warm, garlicky, salty, and cheesy . . . these mouthwatering biscuits pair perfectly with soups, chilis, and stews. You can also use them to make extra-tasty breakfast and lunch sandwiches. Biscuits are usually loaded with butter, but here I use significantly less, and I added some Greek yogurt to the mix. You can double or triple the recipe as needed (and trust me, your family will thank you!).

In a medium bowl, combine the flour, baking powder, and salt and stir with a fork. Cut in 1 tablespoon of the butter with a fork until no longer visible. Add the yogurt, cheddar, and half of the garlic and stir. Turn the dough out onto a lightly floured surface and knead until smooth. Form the dough into 4 biscuits, slightly flattened to a ½-inch thickness.

Spritz the tops of the biscuits and the air fryer basket with oil. Place the biscuits in the air fryer basket and cook at 280°F until golden, 16 to 17 minutes (no need to flip). Transfer the biscuits to a wire rack to cool slightly.

Meanwhile, in a small skillet, melt the remaining 1 tablespoon butter over low heat. Add the remaining garlic and sauté until fragrant, about 1 minute.

Brush the tops of the biscuits with the melted garlic butter and top with the parsley. Serve warm.

PER SERVING: **1 biscuit** • CALORIES **186** • FAT **5 g** • SATURATED FAT **3 g** • CHOLESTEROL **16 mg** • CARBOHYDRATE **26 g** • FIBER **1 g** • PROTEIN **8 g** • SUGARS **1 g** • SODIUM **484 mg**

CRISPY POLENTA ROUNDS
WITH BASIL OIL

SERVES 6

Crisp on the outside and creamy in the center, air-fried polenta makes an easy, tasty side. Tubed polenta is so convenient; just slice it and fry it. This simple garlicky basil oil is my favorite topping, but you could also add some diced cherry tomatoes. Tubed polenta is usually found in either the refrigerated section near the tofu, or in the pasta section.

BASIL OIL

½ cup packed fresh basil leaves, stemmed and rinsed

2 garlic cloves, peeled

¼ teaspoon kosher salt

⅛ teaspoon crushed red pepper flakes

¼ cup extra-virgin olive oil

POLENTA

1 (18-ounce) tube prepared polenta, sliced into eighteen ¼-inch-thick rounds

Olive oil spray

Kosher salt

FOR THE BASIL OIL: In a small food processor, combine the basil, garlic, salt, and pepper flakes and pulse a few times until finely chopped. Add the oil and 1 tablespoon water and pulse 4 to 5 times until smooth.

FOR THE POLENTA: Spritz the polenta rounds with oil and season each one with a pinch of salt.

Working in batches if needed, add the polenta rounds to the air fryer basket in a single layer. Cook at 400°F until crisp, 10 to 16 minutes, flipping halfway through.

Transfer the polenta to a platter, drizzle with basil oil, and serve warm.

PER SERVING: **3 rounds** • CALORIES **141** • FAT **9 g** • SATURATED FAT **1 g** • CHOLESTEROL **0 mg** • CARBOHYDRATE **13 g** • FIBER **1 g** • PROTEIN **2 g** • SUGARS **1 g** • SODIUM **521 mg**

RED CURRY ROASTED EGGPLANT

SERVES 4

1 large eggplant, cut into 1-inch cubes

2 tablespoons extra-virgin olive oil

2 tablespoons Thai red curry paste*

2 tablespoons soy sauce or gluten-free tamari

Olive oil spray

Lime wedges, for serving (optional)

*Read the label to be sure this product is gluten-free.

The quickest way to elevate (almost) any vegetable is to roast it at high heat, and that's exactly what I did here with eggplant in the air fryer. The result is beautiful, caramelized edges on the outside, with plump, juicy flesh on the inside, and the flavor bursts in your mouth! Thai red curry paste mixed with soy sauce is such a simple combination that takes the roasted eggplant to a new level. This is great as a side dish, or even a meatless main served with coconut rice and a squeeze of lime.

In a large bowl, toss the eggplant, olive oil, curry paste, and soy sauce together to coat.

Spritz the air fryer basket with oil. Working in batches if needed, add the eggplant to the air fryer basket in a single layer. Cook at 400°F until caramelized and tender inside, 10 to 12 minutes, shaking the basket halfway through.

Transfer the eggplant to a platter and serve with lime wedges, if desired.

PER SERVING: **4 ounces** · CALORIES **104** · FAT **7 g** · SATURATED FAT **1 g** · CHOLESTEROL **0 mg** · CARBOHYDRATE **8 g** · FIBER **4.5 g** · PROTEIN **2 g** · SUGARS **3 g** · SODIUM **596 mg**

BROCCOLINI
WITH CAESAR-ISH DRESSING

SERVES 4

2 bunches broccolini
(1 pound total)

2 tablespoons plus 1 teaspoon
extra-virgin olive oil

2 to 3 anchovy fillets
(preferably packed in
oil), finely minced

Juice of 1 small lemon

2 tablespoons freshly
grated Parmesan cheese

1 small garlic clove, grated

Pinch of crushed red
pepper flakes

If you toss your veggies with a little water and fill the air fryer basket full (rather than cooking them in a single layer), the vegetables will steam with slightly charred edges. I used that method here for perfectly cooked broccolini and finished it with a simple dressing made with ingredients you'd find in Caesar dressing—lemon juice, olive oil, anchovies, garlic, and Parmesan cheese. This side dish is great served warm or cold.

Trim 1 inch off the ends of the broccolini. If the spears are thicker than a pencil, cut in half lengthwise.

In a large bowl, toss the broccolini with 1 teaspoon of the oil and 2 tablespoons water.

Transfer to the air fryer basket all in one batch. Cook at 370°F until the stems are tender-crisp and the florets slightly charred, 6 to 8 minutes, shaking the basket halfway through.

In a small bowl, whisk together the remaining 2 tablespoons oil, the anchovies, lemon juice, Parmesan, garlic, and pepper flakes until combined.

Transfer the broccolini to a platter, top with the dressing, and serve.

PER SERVING: **4 ounces** · CALORIES **124** · FAT **10 g** · SATURATED FAT **1.5 g** · CHOLESTEROL **5 mg** · CARBOHYDRATE **7 g** · FIBER **3 g** · PROTEIN **3 g** · SUGARS **1 g** · SODIUM **164 mg**

SAVORY SWEET POTATO WEDGES

SERVES 2

¾ teaspoon smoked paprika

½ teaspoon kosher salt

½ teaspoon garlic powder

¼ teaspoon onion powder

Freshly ground black pepper

2 medium sweet potatoes
(6 ounces each), peeled

2 teaspoons extra-
virgin olive oil

Olive oil spray

Sour cream and chives,
for dipping (optional)

Sweet potatoes seasoned with spices is the perfect mix of savory and sweet. Cutting the potatoes into wedges is the quickest way to prepare these, and in the air fryer they come out perfectly tender on the inside every time. I used my favorite blend of spices, and these wedges go with just about everything from burgers, chops, and steaks, such as my Gouda-Stuffed Beef and Mushroom Burgers (page 103), Juicy Brined Pork Chops (page 104), or Rosemary Flank Steak (page 99).

In a medium bowl, combine the smoked paprika, salt, garlic powder, onion powder, and black pepper to taste.

Slice each potato in half, then cut each half into 4 wedges. Place the wedges in the bowl of spices and drizzle with the oil. Toss to evenly coat.

Spritz the air fryer basket with oil. Working in batches if needed, place the potatoes in a single layer without overcrowding the basket. Cook at 380°F until golden brown and crisp on the outside and tender on the inside, 9 to 10 minutes, flipping halfway through.

Serve with the sour cream and chives on the side, if desired.

PER SERVING: **8 wedges** · CALORIES **192** · FAT **5 g** · SATURATED FAT **0.5 g** · CHOLESTEROL **0 mg** · CARBOHYDRATE **36 g** · FIBER **5.5 g** · PROTEIN **3 g** · SUGARS **7 g** · SODIUM **375 mg**

LEMON POTATOES

SERVES 4

1 pound russet potatoes (about 2 medium), cut into ½-inch cubes

2 tablespoons extra-virgin olive oil

1 teaspoon kosher salt

½ teaspoon garlic powder

Freshly ground black pepper

Olive oil spray

½ teaspoon grated lemon zest

1 tablespoon chopped fresh parsley

It's hard to stop eating these lemon potatoes once you start, and they're the perfect side dish to steaks, lamb chops, fish, or just about anything else you can think of. I keep the skins on for added nutrients, which are concentrated in the outer skin.

In a medium bowl, combine the potatoes, oil, salt, garlic powder, and black pepper to taste.

Spritz the air fryer basket with oil. Working in batches as needed, add the potatoes to the air fryer basket in a single layer. Cook at 350°F until golden, about 15 minutes, flipping with a spatula halfway through.

Top with the lemon zest and parsley and serve.

PER SERVING: ¾ cup · CALORIES **151** · FAT **7 g** · SATURATED FAT **1 g** · CHOLESTEROL **0 mg** · CARBOHYDRATE **21 g** · FIBER **1.5 g** · PROTEIN **3 g** · SUGARS **1 g** · SODIUM **287 mg**

BALSAMIC BRUSSELS SPROUTS

SERVES 4

1 pound Brussels sprouts, halved (or quartered, if very large)

2 tablespoons extra-virgin olive oil

¼ teaspoon kosher salt

¼ teaspoon crushed red pepper flakes

1 tablespoon balsamic vinegar

In the last few years, fried Brussels sprouts have become a menu staple at so many restaurants. Of course, deep-frying them doesn't yield the healthiest results, so here I used the air fryer to make a faux-fried version that tastes just as decadent, and with no mess.

In a large bowl, toss the Brussels sprouts with 1 tablespoon of the olive oil, the salt, and pepper flakes.

Working in two batches, place the Brussels sprouts in the air fryer basket in a single layer. Cook at 370°F, shaking the basket a few times, until the sprouts are charred on the outside and tender on the inside, about 10 minutes.

Transfer the Brussels sprouts to a serving dish and dress with the remaining 1 tablespoon olive oil and the balsamic vinegar. Serve immediately.

PER SERVING: **4 ounces** • CALORIES **112** • FAT **7 g** • SATURATED FAT **1 g** • CHOLESTEROL **0 mg** • CARBOHYDRATE **11 g** • FIBER **4.5 g** • PROTEIN **4 g** • SUGARS **3 g** • SODIUM **99 mg**

CONVENTIONAL OVEN COOKING CHART

If you want to make the recipes in this book in your conventional oven instead of an air fryer, I've provided the following cook times and oven temperatures. Keep in mind that the results won't be as crisp as they would be if cooked in the air fryer, but this guide should get you close. Unless noted otherwise, all recipes are cooked on a sheet pan lightly spritzed with oil.

	RECIPE	PAGE	OVEN TEMP	COOK TIME
VEGGIE MAINS	Veggie-Loaded Stromboli	14	425°F	15 to 20 minutes
	Sesame-Soy Tofu Broccoli Bowls	16	400°F	25 minutes, flipping a few times
	Herby Tofu Summer Rolls with Peanut Sauce	19	400°F	25 minutes, flipping a few times
	Big Green Salad with Crispy Spiced Chickpeas and Halloumi	20	375°F for the chickpeas; 450°F for the Halloumi	Cook the chickpeas for 35 to 45 minutes, shaking every 10 minutes. Cook the Halloumi for 4 to 6 minutes.
	Eggplant Parmesan	23	425°F	18 to 20 minutes, flipping halfway
	Un-fried Falafel	24	400°F	22 to 24 minutes, flipping halfway
	Loaded Black Bean Nachos	27	350°F	16 to 18 minutes, flipping halfway. Add the cheese and cook for 4 to 6 minutes more.
	Giant Samosas with Cilantro-Mint Chutney	28	425°F	16 to 18 minutes
	Cheesy Calzones	30	425°F	15 to 20 minutes
	General Tso's Cauliflower	33	400°F	20 to 22 minutes, flipping halfway
	Veggie French Bread Pizzas	34	425°F	8 minutes
	Cajun Arancini with Roasted Red Pepper Marinara	37	400°F	Cook the peppers and onions for 20 minutes, flipping halfway. Cook the arancini for 18 minutes (no need to flip).
POULTRY	Chicken Plantain Sandwich (Jibarito de Pollo)	40	–	For the plantain, cut the ends off and cut a slit along the length of the plantain skin. Microwave the whole plantain (skin on) for 4 to 5 minutes. Carefully peel. Press the plantain to flatten, dip in the seasoned water, spray both sides with oil, and cook in a skillet over medium heat, 5 to 6 minutes per side. Remove and cook the chicken in the skillet over medium-high, about 2 minutes per side.
	Pistachio-Crusted Chicken Cutlets	42	400°F	8 minutes, flipping halfway
	Honey Mustard Chicken Tenders	45	425°F	20 to 24 minutes, flipping halfway
	My Signature Wings	46	425°F	45 minutes, flipping halfway
	Cajun-Spiced Fried Chicken	49	400°F	45 minutes, flipping halfway
	Chicken Caprese	50	Broil	Cook inches from the flame for 5 minutes. Flip and cook for 2 minutes more. Add the cheese and cook for 1 to 2 minutes to melt.
	Latin Roast Chicken (Pollochón)	53	425°F	55 to 60 minutes, or until the internal temperature is 165°F
	Chicken Satay Lettuce Wraps with Peanut Sauce	54	–	Cook in a grill pan over high heat, 3 to 4 minutes on each side.
	Jalapeño-Cheddar Turkey Burgers	57	–	Cook on a grill or in a grill pan over medium heat, 5 to 6 minutes on each side.

RECIPE	PAGE	OVEN TEMP	COOK TIME
Argentinian Sausage Sandwich with Chimichurri (Choripán)	58	425°F	20 to 25 minutes
Juicy Chicken Breasts	61	350°F	Preheat an ovenproof skillet over high heat for 5 minutes until very hot. Place the chicken on the hot skillet and cook for 1 minute per side. Transfer to the oven and bake until the chicken is cooked through, 8 to 10 minutes.
Korean-Style Chicken Rice Bowls with Napa Slaw	62	–	Cook in a grill pan over high heat, 2 to 3 minutes on each side.
Soy-Glazed Boneless Chicken Thighs	65	425°F	30 to 35 minutes, flipping halfway
Kielbasa, Veggie, and Pierogi Dinner	66	425°F	20 to 25 minutes, flipping halfway
Sausage and Pepper Egg Rolls	69	425°F	Bake the sausage, onion, and peppers until cooked through and tender, about 20 minutes. Fill the egg rolls and bake until golden on both sides, 15 to 20 minutes.
Swedish Turkey Meatballs	70	425°F	16 to 20 minutes
Hawaiian BBQ-Inspired Drumsticks	73	425°F	45 to 55 minutes, flipping halfway. Brush with sauce and cook for 1 to 2 minutes more.
Feta-Brined Stuffed Chicken Breasts	74	425°F	20 to 24 minutes (add the cheese in the last 5 minutes)
Honey Sriracha Chicken and Vegetables	77	375°F	Bake the chicken 15 minutes. Flip, add veggies, and cook 15 to 20 minutes more.
One-Pot Balsamic Chicken, Asparagus, and Burst Tomatoes	78	425°F	Cook the chicken, asparagus, and tomatoes for 15 minutes. Toss, add the remaining ingredients, and cook 10 minutes more.
Roasted Turkey Breast	81	375°F	50 to 60 minutes, or until the internal temperature reaches 160° to 165°F
Spicy Fried Chicken Crunch Wraps	82	450°F	25 to 28 minutes, flipping halfway
Chicken-Fried Steak with Sage Gravy	86	–	Cook in a nonstick skillet over medium-high heat, 3 minutes on each side.
Spice-Rubbed Lamb Chops with Cucumbers and Yogurt	88	–	Heat a skillet over medium heat. Spritz the skillet with oil and cook the chops for 4 minutes. Flip and cook for 3 to 4 minutes more, or until the internal temperature reaches 135°F for medium-rare.
Beef Tataki with Ginger-Lemon Dressing	91	–	Cook in a grill pan or skillet over medium-high heat for 9 to 10 minutes, flipping halfway, for medium-rare.
Prosciutto-Wrapped Pork Tenderloin with Fig-Mustard Sauce	92	400°F	24 to 26 minutes
Steak, Potato, and Poblano Burritos	95	400°F	Cook the potatoes on a sheet pan for 28 to 30 minutes, flipping halfway. Cook the steak in a skillet over high heat for 10 to 12 minutes, flipping halfway, for medium-rare.
Cheeseburger-Loaded Fries	96	425°F for the burger; 400°F for the fries	Cook the burger for 12 minutes, flipping halfway. Cook the fries for 18 to 20 minutes, flipping halfway.
Rosemary Flank Steak with Panko Onion Rings	99	–	Cook in a skillet over high heat for 10 to 12 minutes, flipping halfway, for medium-rare.
Pork Milanese with Tricolore Salad	100	425°F	12 to 15 minutes, flipping halfway
Gouda-Stuffed Beef and Mushroom Burgers	103	425°F	Cook the mushrooms for 6 to 8 minutes, flipping halfway. Cook the burgers for 12 minutes, flipping halfway.
Juicy Brined Pork Chops	104	425°F	15 to 20 minutes, flipping halfway, or until the internal temperature reaches 145°F.

POULTRY

BEEF, PORK & LAMB

RECIPE	PAGE	OVEN TEMP	COOK TIME
Beef and Broccoli	106	—	Cook the beef in a skillet over high heat for 3 minutes. Add the broccoli and cook for 4 to 5 minutes more.
Lamb Loin Chops with Pistachio-Mint Gremolata	108	—	Cook in a grill pan or skillet over medium-high heat for 9 to 10 minutes, flipping halfway, for medium-rare.
Steak Fajitas	111	—	Cook the steak in a skillet over medium-high heat for 9 to 10 minutes, flipping halfway, for medium-rare. Cook the vegetables over medium-low heat for 10 minutes, until tender.
Mustard-Dill Salmon with Asparagus	114	425°F	10 to 12 minutes, flipping halfway
King Crab Legs with Garlic-Lemon Butter	117	—	Steam in a pot of boiling water for 10 to 15 minutes, until heated through in the center.
Sesame-Crusted Tuna with Wasabi Mayo	118	—	Heat a skillet over medium-high heat. Sear the tuna on the first side for 3 minutes. Flip and cook for 2 to 3 minutes more for medium-rare.
Bacon-Wrapped Scallops	121	Broil	Place the scallops on a broiler pan set 6 inches from the flame. Cook for 12 minutes, flipping two or three times to prevent the bacon from burning.
Shrimp Tempura Sushi "Burritos"	122	425°F	15 to 18 minutes, flipping halfway
Fried Catfish and Hushpuppies with Creamy Slaw	124	425°F	Cook the fish for 10 to 12 minutes, flipping halfway. Cook the hushpuppies for 14 to 16 minutes.
Cajun Shrimp Dinner	126	—	Cook in a skillet over high heat in two batches, 5 to 8 minutes per batch.
Blackened Fish Tacos	129	—	Cook in a skillet over medium heat, 4 to 5 minutes on each side.
Fried Shrimp Po'Boy Wraps	130	425°F	8 minutes
Gnocchi with Shrimp and Burst Tomatoes	133	450°F	10 to 12 minutes, flipping halfway (use two sheet pans)
Sweet and Spicy Glazed Salmon	134	425°F	10 to 12 minutes, flipping halfway
Fried Fish Fillet Sandwiches	136	425°F	12 to 14 minutes, flipping halfway
Lobster Tails with Garlic-Paprika Butter	138	350°F	15 minutes
Tzatziki Fish Tacos	140	375°F	10 to 15 minutes, depending on the thickness
Golden Breaded Cauliflower	144	450°F	15 to 18 minutes
Smashed Potatoes	147	425°F	After smashing the potatoes, cook for 20 minutes.
Blistered Asian-Style Green Beans	148	450°F	15 to 18 minutes, stirring halfway
Cheesy Broccoli Potato Patties	151	—	Spritz a skillet with oil and cook the patties over medium-high heat for 3 minutes on each side, until golden.
Roasted Balsamic Asparagus	152	425°F	10 to 12 minutes, flipping halfway
Mushrooms with Frizzled Shallots and Bacon	155	425°F	26 to 28 minutes, flipping halfway
Eggplant Fries	156	450°F	10 minutes. Flip and cook 5 minutes more.
Garlic Cheddar Biscuits	159	375°F	20 minutes on the top rack. Let cool for 10 minutes.
Crispy Polenta Rounds with Basil Oil	160	450°F	20 to 24 minutes, flipping halfway
Red Curry Roasted Eggplant	163	450°F	10 to 12 minutes, flipping halfway
Broccolini with Caesar-ish Dressing	164	400°F	20 to 25 minutes
Savory Sweet Potato Wedges	167	425°F	25 to 30 minutes
Lemon Potatoes	168	400°F	28 to 30 minutes, flipping halfway
Balsamic Brussels Sprouts	170	425°F	20 minutes, stirring halfway

SEAFOOD

SIDES

INDEX

Note: Page references in *italics* indicate photographs.

ACKNOWLEDGMENTS

First off, the biggest thank-you to the Skinnytaste family and to my dedicated fans—who allow me to continue doing this dream job.

So many wonderful people are involved in making a cookbook happen. A heartfelt thank-you to everyone involved who put this air fryer cookbook together.

To my family, who are always so supportive and gladly willing to act as my taste testers. Thank you for loving me so much!

My very good friend Heather K. Jones, RD, how is it possible this is our sixth cookbook together?! Your positive energy makes this whole process less stressful. . . . Thank you for always inspiring me. And to Heather's team—Danielle Hazard, Donna Fennessy, and Jackie Price—thanks for paying attention to all the details.

To my aunt Ligia Caldas, who keeps me organized, I couldn't do it without you.

To my agent, Janis Donnaud, I am eternally grateful we found each other.

To everyone at Clarkson Potter, including Jenn Sit, Erica Gelbard, Stephanie Davis, Jenny Beal Davis, Stephanie Huntwork, and Lydia O'Brien—I love working with you all.

I am so grateful for my talented photographer, Aubrie Pick, and her team.

And last but not least, to all my girlfriends. Thank you for always supporting me, sharing your recipes and ideas, or just joining me for a glass of wine.

Published in the United States by Clarkson Potter/Publishers, an imprint of Random House, a division of Penguin Random House LLC, New York.
clarksonpotter.com

CLARKSON POTTER is a trademark and POTTER with colophon is a registered trademark of Penguin Random House LLC.

Library of Congress Cataloging-in-Publication Data
Names: Homolka, Gina, author. | Jones, Heather K., author. | Pick, Aubrie, other. Title: Skinnytaste air fryer dinners : 75 healthy recipes for easy weeknight meals / by Gina Homolka with Heather K. Jones, R.D. ; photographs by Aubrie Pick. Description: New York : Clarkson Potter, [2021] | Includes index. Identifiers: LCCN 2021028443 (print) | LCCN 2021028444 (ebook) | ISBN 9780593235607 (ebook) | ISBN 9780593235591 (hardcover) Subjects: LCSH: Hot air frying. | Roasting (Cooking) | Suppers. | LCGFT: Cookbooks. Classification: LCC TX689 (ebook) | LCC TX689 .H663 2021 (print) | DDC 641.7/7—dc23LC record available at https://lccn.loc.gov/2021028443

ISBN 978-0-593-23559-1
Ebook ISBN 978-0-593-23560-7

Printed in the United States

Photographer: Aubrie Pick
Prop Stylist: Claire Mack
Food Stylist: Emily Caneer
Food Stylist Assistant: Huxley McCorkle
Photo Assistant: Patrick Aguilar
Editor: Jennifer Sit
Assistant Editor: Lydia O'Brien
Designer: Jennifer K. Beal Davis
Production Editor: Patricia Shaw
Production Manager: Kim Tyner
Compositors: Merri Ann Morrell and Nick Patton
Copy Editor: Kate Slate
Indexer: Elizabeth T. Parson
Marketer: Stephanie Davis
Publicist: Erica Gelbard

First Edition

1st Printing